DEDICATED
TO ALL TIN CAN SAILORS

. . . MAY THEY REST IN PEACE FOREVER,
THOSE THAT DIED. AND MAY GOD BLESS
AND GRANT PEACE FOREVER TO THOSE
THAT LIVE.

SJG

For my friend Sam,
With, as always, great
respect and admiration.
– Alan Barnard

Artwork by Alan Barnard

A SAILOR'S STORY

Written and Illustrated by
Sam Glanzman

Foreword by Max Brooks
Introduction by Larry Hama
Afterword by Chuck Dixon

DOVER PUBLICATIONS, INC.
Mineola, New York

Dover Publications would like to warmly acknowledge the contribution made by Steve Fears in assisting in the organization and completion of A Sailor's Story .

Color correction of artwork by Frank M. Cuonzo

Bibliographical Note

A Sailor's Story, first published by Dover Publications, Inc., in 2015, is an unabridged republication of the following works originally published by Marvel Comics, New York: *A Sailor's Story* (1987) and *A Sailor's Story, Book Two: Winds, Dreams, and Dragons* (1989). The artwork has been color corrected to closer reflect the author's original vision. A new Foreword, Introduction, and Afterword have been specially written for the Dover edition.

International Standard Book Number

ISBN-13: 978-0-486-79812-7
ISBN-10: 0-486-79812-7

Manufactured in the United States by Courier Corporation
79812701   2015
www.doverpublications.com

Foreword

Max Brooks

"Winds, Dreams, and Dragons" is the second book of Sam Glanzman's "A Sailor's Story" series and the first one I stumbled across back in the summer of 1987. What immediately drew me to this story of a WWII tin can sailor was not the drama of combat, but the specific lack of it. Unlike most men of my Generation-X, I had a father who was active in World War II. I grew up on his stories of daily life in the Army: cooking in his helmet, keeping his toes warm, having to blast a fox hole from ground too hard for entrenching tools. Those little details were my bridge to that distant time. They made the war accessible. They allowed me to picture myself in a similar situation, because, while I had no idea what it was like to have to face enemy fire (and still don't!), I can identify with the goal of a decent meal and a good night's rest.

Like my father's stories, the simple human details of "A Sailor's Story" gave me a unique, personal look into a conflict that is as far from my existence as the Battle for Middle Earth. I learned that sailors lived on coffee, that their letters were censored, and that sometimes their most tantalizing fantasy was of "an American cheese sandwich on a hard roll and an ice cold Coca-Cola." In "Winds, Dreams, and Dragons" the running story is of Glanzman just trying to find a cool place to sleep. He tries the bow but ends up "drenched to the skin and freezing." He tries underneath the gun mount but is slammed against the steel when the gun is unexpectedly fired. He tries sleeping on the searchlight platform way up at the smoke stack, only to be drenched in soot when the engines blast out their accumulated muck.

In addition to daily life, Glanzman breaks down life aboard a U.S. Navy destroyer with clear, concise, Clancy-esque explanations. He breaks down every aspect of this remarkable machine, from a "Fireroom" schematic in the first book to an entire ship diagram in the second. One piece of information that never left me was that the armor on the ship's gun mounts was so thin that even rifle fire could penetrate it! It is in his simplicity that I could truly appreciate the complex tasks hoisted upon these young men (some of whom were only paid 3 cents an hour!)

For me the most poignant moment in both books comes when the crew of Glanzman's ship, the USS Stevens, waits for their mail sack to be lowered across from another ship. By this point, Glanzman has done such a masterful job of describing the isolation of the these men that when the rope breaks, the bag sinks, and the men ". . . just stood there . . . sorta numb," your heart can't help but break for them.

If you want to know what life was like for members of the "Greatest Generation," who served their country aboard small ships in a big ocean, this is it. No one, from Stephen Ambrose to Steven Spielberg, can tell a better story than "A Sailor's Story."

Artwork by Sam Glanzman

Introduction
Larry Hama

I take inordinate and wholly undeserved pride in having been the editor of record of the Marvel graphic novel *A Sailor's Story*, written and drawn by Sam Glanzman. My biggest contribution to the project was picking up the phone and telling Sam, "Go ahead and do it." Pat Redding Scanlon, my diligently capable assistant editor, did the hands-on production work, proofing, and all of the traffic; I remember her opening a box of original pages when they came in from Sam and remarking, "It's like an honor just to hold the pages." Phil Felix, the letterer, said pretty much the same thing. And it *was* an honor, for any number of reasons.

It was an honor because Sam Glanzman wasn't just doing a fancy comic book—he was testifying, and memorializing. He was writing a history that wasn't in the logbooks and naval journals. He was bearing witness from the mess deck, not from the bridge. He was doing all that with the simultaneous voices of a nineteen-year-old and a septuagenarian, somehow combining the awe and wonder seen through the teen's eyes, but related with the wisdom and compassion gained by years of introspection.

By the time Sam started working on *A Sailor's Story* he had already been honing his graphic storytelling skills for close to four decades. There are no flashy effects, bizarre angles, or other tricks to jazz up the page. It's just straightforward, clear storytelling about characters whose humanity is conveyed with grace and sly wit. What more can you ask for?

There are many books about the U.S. Navy in the South Pacific during WWII, but no other graphic novels, to my knowledge, written and drawn by somebody who had actually been there. Somebody who meticulously chronicled all that he saw in sketchbooks and diaries. Somebody who could remember the sights, the sounds, the smells, the joys and the sorrows, the fear and the boredom—and who had the power to translate it all into pictures and words that will inform you, move you, and stay with you in the way that all good stories do.

A SAILOR'S STORY

CONTENTS

A SAILOR'S STORY
BOOK I

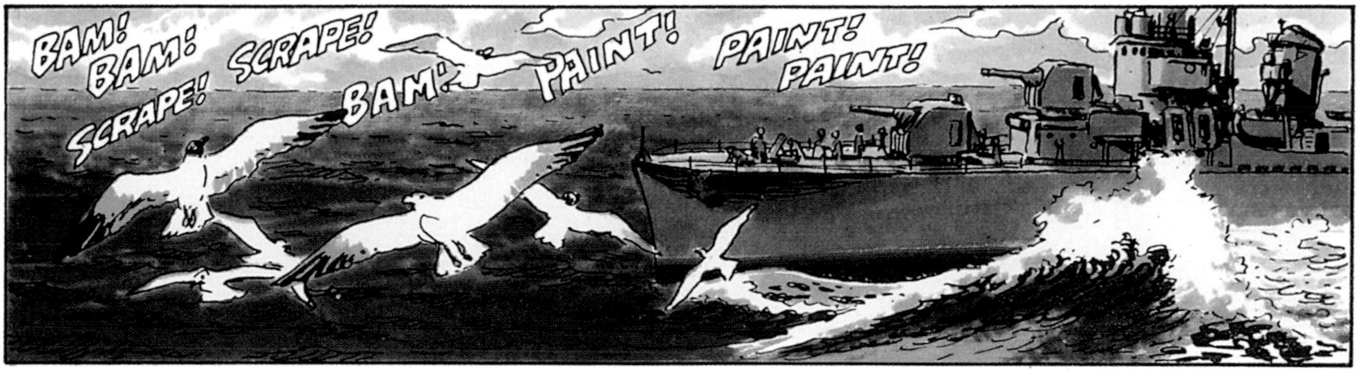
BAM!
BAM!
SCRAPE!
SCRAPE!
BAM!
PAINT!
PAINT!
PAINT!

DECEMBER 1941

I HAD JUST TURNED 17 AND WAS LIVING IN UPSTATE NEW YORK WHEN TWO DAYS AFTER MY BIRTHDAY, PEARL HARBOR WAS STRUCK.

A YEAR WOULD PASS BEFORE I WOULD BE OLD ENOUGH TO ENLIST.

THAT YEAR OF WAITING (1941-1942) WAS FILLED WITH A SEEMINGLY ENDLESS CHAIN OF DEFEATS FOR THE ALLIES IN THE PACIFIC. JAPAN GOBBLED UP ISLANDS AND TERRITORY LIKE PAC-MAN ON A RAMPAGE.

JAPAN'S EMPIRE AT ITS HEIGHT
AUGUST 1942

Russia

Japan

China

GUAM--DEC. 10, 1941.

WAKE--DEC. 23, 1941.

HONG KONG--DEC. 25, 1941.

Philippines

MANILA--JAN. 2, 1942.

Borneo

BATAAN--APRIL 9, 1942.

CORREGIDOR--MAY 6, 1942.

SINGAPORE
FEB. 15, 1942.

New Guinea

NETHERLANDS EAST INDIES--MARCH 7, 1942.

389

HALF OF OUR PACIFIC FLEET HAD BEEN DESTROYED AT PEARL HARBOR. WITH NO STRONG OFFENSIVE FLEET, GIVEN THE OVERWHELMING SUPERIORITY OF THE JAPANESE THE ALLIES COULD ONLY REACT, OR BE CONTENT TO HIT AND RUN AND HIDE.

DECEMBER 1942

BY NOW I WAS 18. I HAD BEEN ORPHANED AT AN EARLY AGE AND LIVED ALONE. MY ONLY COMPANION WAS A BLACK LABRADOR DOG I CALLED "BEAUTY". NOW, OLD ENOUGH TO ENLIST, I HAD TO LEAVE BEAUTY BEHIND WITH A GOOD FRIEND AND NEIGHBOR...IF YOU HAVE EVER BEEN ALONE IN LIFE AND ARE A DOG LOVER YOU MUST KNOW HOW SAD MY DEPARTURE FROM HER WAS.

OKAY, PETE... THANKS!

BYE BEAUTY!

I'LL TAKE GOOD CARE OF HER, SAM!

AFTER SIX WEEKS OF BOOT CAMP I REQUESTED SEA DUTY AND IN THE SPRING OF '43 WAS SENT TO BOSTON WHERE I WAS ASSIGNED A SHIP...IT WAS A DESTROYER. NEVER IN MY LIFE HAD I FELT SUCH PRIDE AND JOY. FROM BOSTON I AND THREE OTHER MEN REPORTED TO NEW YORK TO BECOME SAILORS OF THE U.S.S. STEVENS.

AT THAT TIME SHE WAS IN THE BROOKLYN NAVY YARD BEING REFITTED.

FROM THE DOCK TO THE MIDDLE OF THE SHIP WAS A BRIDGE-LIKE AFFAIR. CROSSING IT WE DID NOT FACE THE BACK OF THE SHIP WHERE A FLAG WAS HANGING FROM THE BACK CHIMNEY NOR DID WE SALUTE, BEFORE I ...

SAILOR!! NEXT TIME FACE THE COLORS ON THE AFT STACK AND GIVE THE PROPER HAND SALUTE AT THE GANGWAY BEFORE BOARDING. AT THE QUARTERDECK, SALUTE THE OFFICER OF THE DECK AND REQUEST PERMISSION TO COME ABOARD.

THE O.D. * AIN'T HERE NOW... I'LL TAKE YOUR PAPERS, ME NAME'S BUCK!

THAT WAS BUCK TALBERT STANDING MESSENGER WATCH, FROM THEN ON I NEVER WENT TO THE BACK OF THE SHIP BUT ALWAYS "AFT", NEVER SALUTED THE FLAG BUT ALWAYS THE "COLORS" AND NEVER CLIMBED THE CHIMNEY BUT ALWAYS THE "STACK"... BUCK TOLD US TO REPORT AFT TO BO'S'N E. SMITH.

* O.D. -- OFFICER OF THE DECK.

MAKING OUR WAY AFT I COULDN'T BELIEVE WHAT I WAS SEEING... NOTHING LIKE THE COMICS OR THE MOVIES. YOU COULDN'T HARDLY MOVE, WORKMEN, SAILORS, PEOPLE AND ...STUFF... ALL OVER THE PLACE. I COULDN'T SEE THE **SHIP**. IT SEEMED EVERY INCH HAD SOMETHING IN, ON, OR WAS BEING TORN OUT OF HER.

HOW COULD ANYONE MOVE MUCH LESS FIGHT... EVERYTHING SEEMED SO CLOSE TOGETHER. BO'S'N E. SMITH WAS ON THE FANTAIL *... HE SHOWED US AROUND... AND GAVE US A LECTURE.

THE FLOORS OF A SHIP ARE ALWAYS *DECKS*; THE WALLS ARE ALWAYS *BULKHEADS*; STAIRS ARE ALWAYS *LADDERS*. THERE ARE NO HALLS OR CORRIDORS IN SHIPS; ONLY *PASSAGEWAYS*... NO CEILINGS IN YOUR ROOM; ONLY THE *OVERHEAD* OF YOUR *COMPARTMENT*. OPENINGS IN THE OUTSIDE OF THE SHIP ARE *PORTS* NOT WINDOWS. OTHER OPENINGS IN DECKS OR BULKHEADS ARE *HATCHES*...

...THAT'S A 20 MM !!

... AN OBJECT DIRECTLY OFF THE SIDE OF YOUR SHIP IS *ABEAM*. AN OBJECT OR LINE RUNNING DIRECTLY ACROSS THE SHIP, LIKE A PASSAGEWAY IS *ATHWART-SHIPS*. WHEN YOU STAND AT THE CENTER OF THE SHIP YOU ARE *AMIDSHIPS*...

...THAT'S A 40 MM !!

WHEN YOU FACE EITHER SIDE YOU FACE *OUT-BOARD*. YOUR SHIP-MATE AT THE RAIL WHO LOOKS BACK AT YOU IS FACING *IN-BOARD*. AN OBJECT OVER YOUR HEAD IS *ABOVE*; AN OBJECT BENEATH YOU IS *BELOW*...

I TRIED TO ACT NON-CHALANT GOING DOWN THE LADDER...

YIEEKS!

IN ROUGH WEATHER YOU DON'T SHUT THE WINDOWS AND LOCK THE DOORS; YOU *CLOSE THE PORTS* AND *DOG THE HATCHES*. A PICTURE IS NEVER NAILED TO THE WALL; IT IS *SECURED* TO THE *BULKHEAD*. YOU DON'T MOP THE FLOOR; YOU *SWAB THE DECK*...

...THIS IS A *HATCH* LEADING *BELOW* TO YOUR COMPARTMENT!

* FANTAIL—THE AFTER SECTION OF THE MAIN DECK ON DESTROYERS AND CRUISERS.

4

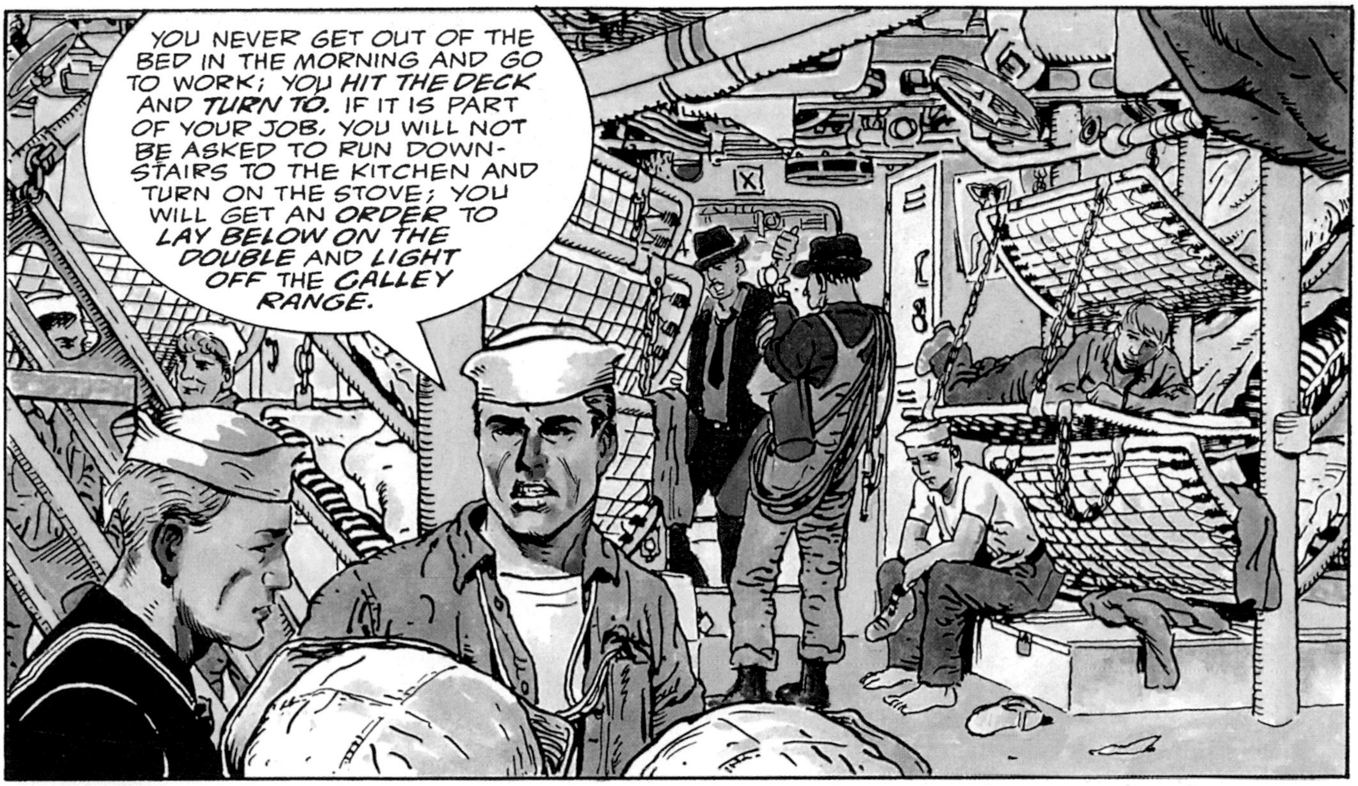
YOU NEVER GET OUT OF THE BED IN THE MORNING AND GO TO WORK; YOU **HIT THE DECK** AND **TURN TO.** IF IT IS PART OF YOUR JOB, YOU WILL NOT BE ASKED TO RUN DOWN-STAIRS TO THE KITCHEN AND TURN ON THE STOVE; YOU WILL GET AN **ORDER** TO **LAY BELOW ON THE DOUBLE** AND **LIGHT OFF** THE **GALLEY RANGE.**

BO'S'N E. SMITH ASSIGNED US BUNKS AND LOCKERS, TOLD US WE WERE IN THE DECK'S FIRST DIVISION AND TO REPORT TO OUR DIVISION OFFICER... BO'S'N E. SMITH THEN DISAPPEARED AN' I NEVER AGAIN HEARD HIM SPEAK... EXCEPT TO ISSUE ORDERS.

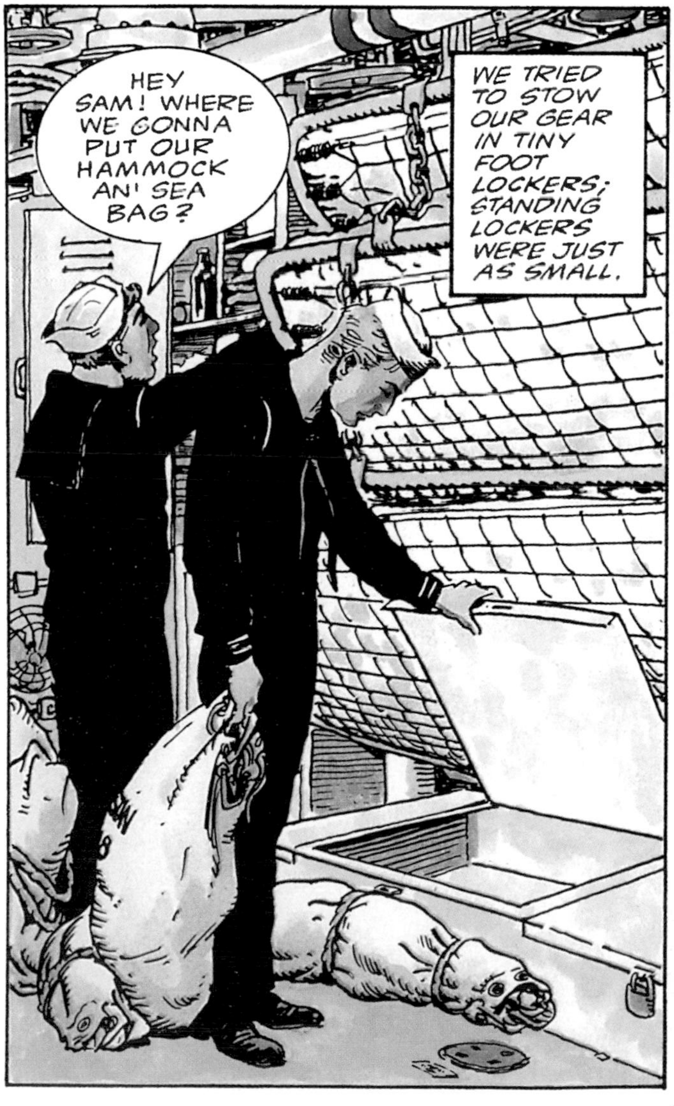
HEY SAM! WHERE WE GONNA PUT OUR HAMMOCK AN' SEA BAG?
WE TRIED TO STOW OUR GEAR IN TINY FOOT LOCKERS; STANDING LOCKERS WERE JUST AS SMALL.

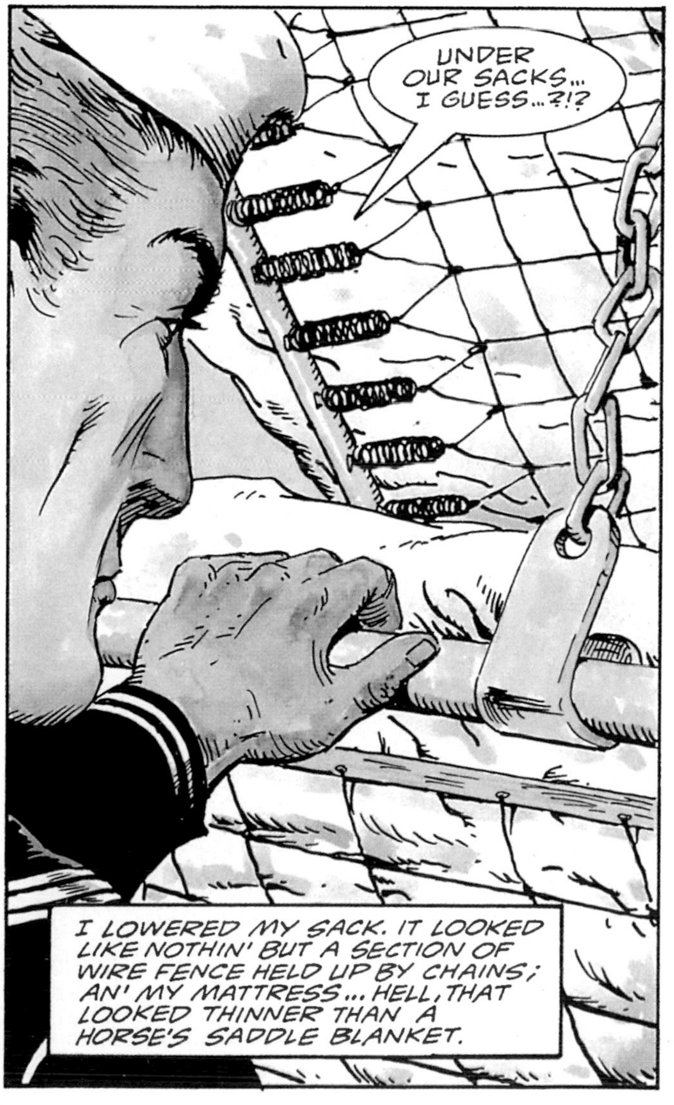
UNDER OUR SACKS... I GUESS...?!?
I LOWERED MY SACK. IT LOOKED LIKE NOTHIN' BUT A SECTION OF WIRE FENCE HELD UP BY CHAINS; AN' MY MATTRESS... HELL, THAT LOOKED THINNER THAN A HORSE'S SADDLE BLANKET.

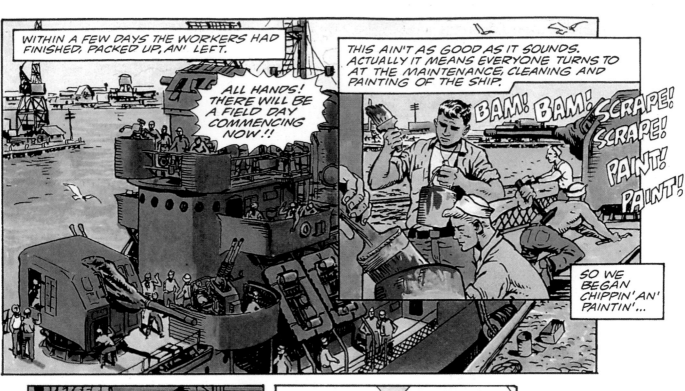

WITHIN A FEW DAYS THE WORKERS HAD FINISHED, PACKED UP, AN' LEFT.

ALL HANDS! THERE WILL BE A FIELD DAY COMMENCING NOW!!

THIS AIN'T AS GOOD AS IT SOUNDS. ACTUALLY IT MEANS EVERYONE TURNS TO AT THE MAINTENANCE, CLEANING AND PAINTING OF THE SHIP.

BAM! BAM! SCRAPE! SCRAPE! PAINT! PAINT!

SO WE BEGAN CHIPPIN' AN' PAINTIN'...

THERE WAS A GUY STICKIN' OUT OF A HATCH...WATCHING US AND LAUGHING...OTHERS SAT AROUND HIM, SMIRKIN' AN' DRINKING COFFEE.

BAM! BAM! SCRAPE! PAINT!

HOW COME YOU GUYS DON'T HAF'TA TURN TO ??

WHO, US ?? ARE YOU KIDDING ? NEVER !! WE'RE SNIPES*... YOU GUYS AIN'T NOTHIN' BUT SEAMEN ... DECK APES!!

SCRAPE! SCRAPE! PAINT!

* SNIPES -- BELOW DECK MEMBERS... ENGINEERS, FIREMEN, WATERTENDERS.

A FEW DAYS LATER WE GOT UNDERWAY AND HEADED OUT TO SEA. MY HEART WAS POUNDING WITH EXCITEMENT, MY MIND WORRIED WITH UNCERTAINTY... WHAT LAY AHEAD ??

DOWN THE WHOLE EASTERN SEABOARD... WHEN WE WEREN'T ON WATCH... WE SEAMEN WERE KEPT BUSY CHIPPIN' AN' PAINTIN'.

BAM! BAM! SCRAPE! SCRAPE! SCRAPE! BAM! PAINT! PAINT! PAINT!

IT WAS GETTING DOWNRIGHT MONOTONOUS... AN' THAT SMART ALECK COXS'N WASN'T NO P&R MAN EITHER.

IS THIS ALL THERE IS ??

DON'T WORRY... YOU'RE GOING ON WATCH SOON!

A BUSY CREW MAKES A HAPPY SHIP! HEE HEE!

AT PANAMA, ENTERING LIMÓN BAY WE TOOK AN 8-MILE LONG CHANNEL TO THE GATUN LOCKS...

...THE LOCKS LOOKING LIKE GIANT STEPS, LIFT A SHIP ABOUT 85 FEET FROM SEA LEVEL TO GATUN LAKE.

HERE AT THE LOCKS OUR ENGINES WERE SHUT DOWN. ALL LARGE SHIPS MUST BE TOWED THROUGH THE LOCKS BY SMALL ELECTRIC LOCOMOTIVES CALLED "MULES".

ABOUT THIS TIME I WAS ON K.P. DUTY. LOOKING OUT THE SPUD LOCKER.* I COULD JUST ABOUT SEE THOSE LITTLE CARS.

* SPUD LOCKER-- A 5 X 5 COMPARTMENT OFF THE GALLEY USED FOR PREPARING VEGETABLES.

7

IT TOOK ABOUT 10 TO 15 MINUTES TO RAISE THE WATER LEVEL IN EACH LOCK. AT THE LAST LOCK THE MULES WERE RELEASED AND UNDER OUR OWN POWER WE ENTERED GATUN LAKE...

...WHICH WAS ABOUT 30 MILES ACROSS. GAILLARD CUT WAS NEXT. THIS MAN-MADE CHANNEL IS ONLY ABOUT 40 FEET DEEP, 9 MILES LONG AND 300 FEET WIDE. NEXT, PEDRO MIGUEL LOCKS... NEXT, MIRA FLORES LAKE AND IT'S LOCKS. FINALLY DOWN ANOTHER CHANNEL TO THE BAY OF PANAMA... AND THE OPEN SEA.

FROM THE ATLANTIC OCEAN TO THE PACIFIC IN A LITTLE OVER 50 MILES, NOT BAD, EH SAM?

YEAH BUCK, OFF THE TOP OF MY HEAD I GUESS IF WE HAD TO GO AROUND THE TIP OF SOUTH AMERICA IT'D BE SOMETHING LIKE 8,000 MILES?

WHAT'RE YOU DOIN'?? SIGHT SEEIN'? GET HOT ON THAT CORN... YOU GOT'TA SLICE THESE TOMATOES NEXT!!

IN 1943 THE U.S.S. STEVENS HAD A SCOUT PLANE... FOR A DESTROYER THIS WAS AS UNCOMMON AS HEN'S TEETH.

THIS... A NAVY EXPERIMENT... DIDN'T WORK OUT... LATER, THE PLANE WAS REMOVED.

WE HAD SOME DRILLS WITH THAT STUPID PLANE...

...SHOOTIN' IT OFF AND HAULING IT ABOARD.

OF COURSE SEAMEN GOT THIS DUTY... SNIPES, AS USUAL, SAT AROUND DRINKING THEIR COFFEE AND LAUGHING.

EASE OFF! HANDSOME NOW!

ONCE... SOMETHING WENT WRONG. THE PLANE MADE A WHIP-SNAP MOTION...

...THE PILOT WAS STRAPPED IN... THE GUNNER WASN'T.

YOU GODDAMN SWABBIES! YOU GODDAMN DECK APES! YOU GODDAMN TIN CAN SAILORS! YOU GODDAM!?! GODDAMS!!

AWAY THE MOTOR WHALE BOAT!

THE GUNNER, SGT. STONE, WASN'T HURT... BUT HIS GOOD FORTUNE DIDN'T AFFECT HIS BAD TEMPER.

BEING AN OFFICER, THE PILOT QUARTERED WITH THE SHIP'S OFFICERS. BUT HIS GUNNER SGT. STONE HAD TO BUNK WITH THE CREW.

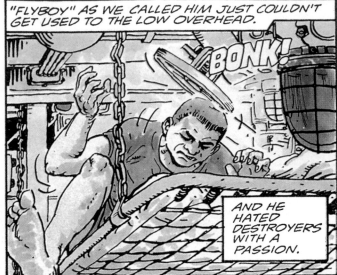

"FLYBOY" AS WE CALLED HIM JUST COULDN'T GET USED TO THE LOW OVERHEAD.

BONK!

AND HE HATED DESTROYERS WITH A PASSION.

OF COURSE WE HAD OUR CHOW LINES. BUT THE CHOW WAS ALWAYS FRESH, HOT... AND I'D SAY EXCELLENT... ALWAYS PLENTY OF COFFEE AND DESSERT.

WHAT'S FER TODAY?

PORK CHOPS AN' BEANS AN' POTATOES ...AND FRESH BAKED BREAD... AND LETTUCE AN' TOMATOES... AND APPLE COBBLER...AND...

SHUT UP!

GALLEY

HOT STUFF !! GANG-WAY !!

MESS HALL, TWO DECKS BELOW.

YOU MIGHT SAY THE SHIP'S HEADS WERE SMALL...BUT SUFFICIENT. THE AFT HEAD HAD A FEW SHOWERS, TOILETS, AND ABOUT TEN SINKS.

HEY ARNOLD! STEVE! YOU EVER BEEN TO HAWAII?

YOU KIDDIN'? I AIN'T NEVER BEEN OUT OF CHASE-VILLE!

THE STEVENS HAD A SHIP'S STORE. NOW THAT WAS SMALL, ABOUT 5 BY 8 FEET. NO SODAS, NO ICE CREAM... JUST CANDY (POGEY BAIT), TOILETRIES, WRITING PAPER, CIGARETTES, CIGARS AND GUM.

WHAT'CHA GOT?

'SIDES NOTHIN'!!

COMBS

SOMETIME IN AUGUST 1943 WE SIGHTED THE HAWAIIAN ISLANDS. HAWAII WAS BEAUTIFUL THEN AND RIGHTFULLY CALLED "THE PEARL OF THE PACIFIC".

PEARL HARBOR IS NOT ON HAWAII BUT ON ONE OF HER LESSER ISLANDS, OAHU.

NOW HEAR THIS! ALL HANDS IN THE LIBERTY SECTION LAY AFT ON THE FANTAIL... DUTY SECTION STAND BY TO RECEIVE THE LIBERTY BOAT!

HERE AT TIN CAN ALLEY WE "NESTED" WITH OTHER CANS.

SALVAGE AND REPAIR WORK WAS STILL GOING ON, ALMOST A YEAR AND A HALF AFTER THE ATTACK.

WHILE ON LIBERTY I DIDN'T GET TO HAWAII OR EVEN WAIKIKI BEACH WHICH IS ON OAHU... REMEMBER THIS WAS IN THE 40'S, THE YOUTH AT THAT TIME WAS NOT SO WORLDLY AS TODAY. YOU MIGHT EVEN SAY WE WERE NAIVE. HONOLULU WAS AN EXOTIC... OPEN CITY TO US... WE WENT CRAZY!

SIGHTSEEING FOR SOME...

I'M GONNA GET ME A LEI!

YOU AIN'T THE ONLY ONE!

BARROOM BRAWLS FOR OTHERS...

AN' PLEASURE PALACES FOR ALL... THE LINES WENT AROUND THE BLOCK...

YOU ASK FOR ME, SAILOR BOY!

ULP!!

RETURNING, WE WERE A DISGUSTING LOT. BUT SOMEHOW, SOMEWAY, WE MANAGED TO REACH THE LIBERTY BOAT ON TIME AND GET BACK ABOARD.

LES' TRY IT AGAIN!

PERMISSION TA BOARD SIR?

GETCHA GODDAMN HANDS OFFA ME!

MY SHOE! MY SHOE! WHO'S GOT MY SHOE?

W-WHER'M I AT??

WAKE UP, JOE!

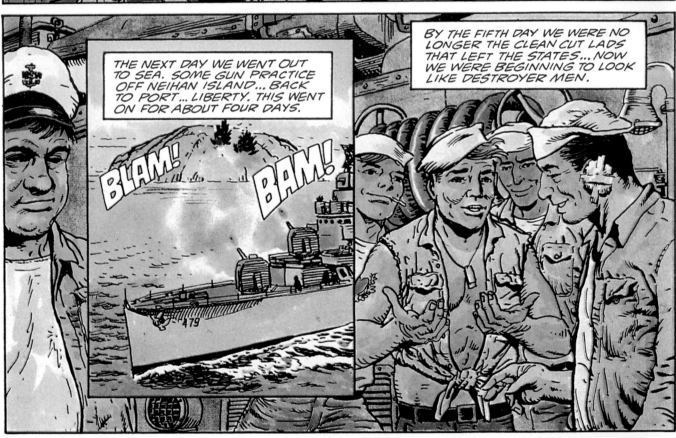

THE NEXT DAY WE WENT OUT TO SEA. SOME GUN PRACTICE OFF NEIHAN ISLAND... BACK TO PORT... LIBERTY. THIS WENT ON FOR ABOUT FOUR DAYS.

BLAM!

BAM!

479

BY THE FIFTH DAY WE WERE NO LONGER THE CLEAN CUT LADS THAT LEFT THE STATES... NOW WE WERE BEGINNING TO LOOK LIKE DESTROYER MEN.

AND BY THE END OF SEPTEMBER WE WOULD BE DESTROYER MEN. FOR ON AUGUST 20 1943...

ALL HANDS! THIS IS THE CAPTAIN SPEAKING! IN A FEW DAYS WE WILL FORM UP WITH A CARRIER TASK GROUP FOR AN AIR STRIKE ON THE ENEMY HELD ISLAND OF MARCUS... WE ARE NOW IN THE WAR!!

NO MORE FIRE PRACTICE AT NEIHAN... WE PASSED IT DOING FLANK SPEED.

WE HAD BEEN STEAMING ALONE WHEN ONE MORNING...

NOW HEAR THIS! THERE WILL BE A G.Q. ALERT AT FIFTEEN HUNDRED HOURS....ALL HANDS WILL SHOWER AND DON CLEAN CLOTHES BEFORE THIRTEEN HUNDRED!

SHOWER? WHAT THE HELL FOR?

TO LESSEN THE CHANCES OF INFECTION....'CASE YOU GET YOUR HEAD BLOWN OFF, DUMMY!

I GOT THE SHOCK OF MY LIFE WHEN I WENT TOPSIDE. WE HAD FORMED UP WITH THE CARRIER TASK GROUP.

WOW!! THERE MUST BE HUNDREDS OF SHIPS OUT THERE!

I DON'T RECALL WHAT SHIPS WERE WITH US, BUT THE CARRIERS ALL HAD THE NEW F6F HELLCAT FIGHTERS. THEY WERE CIRCLING OVERHEAD, GETTING IN FORMATION WITH THE DIVE BOMBERS.

I THINK THAT'S THE YORKTOWN, AN' THAT'S THE HEAVY CRUISER IN--? NO, THAT'S THE MINNEAPOLIS!

I COUNTED FOUR CRUISERS AN' TWENTY FOUR CANS SO FAR!

SURE FEELS GOOD TO HAVE ALL THAT POWER 'ROUND US!

13

WHEN HIS FLOAT PLANE WASN'T ALOFT, SGT. STONE ALSO HAD A SHIPBOARD G.Q. STATION... AT 1500 "FLYBOY" WAS STILL IN THE SHOWER...

ALL HANDS MAN YOUR BATTLE STATIONS FOR G.Q. ALERT!!

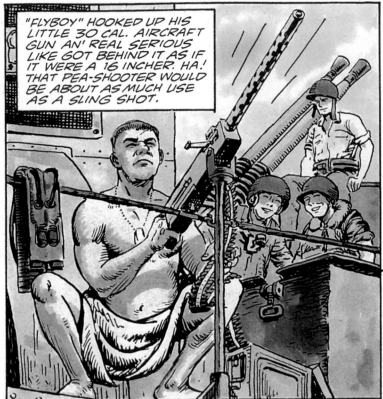

"FLYBOY" HOOKED UP HIS LITTLE 30 CAL. AIRCRAFT GUN AN' REAL SERIOUS LIKE GOT BEHIND IT AS IF IT WERE A 16 INCHER. HA! THAT PEA-SHOOTER WOULD BE ABOUT AS MUCH USE AS A SLING SHOT.

BY NOW ALL CANS WERE WELL OUT IN FRONT, SCREENING FOR THE HEAVIER SHIPS.

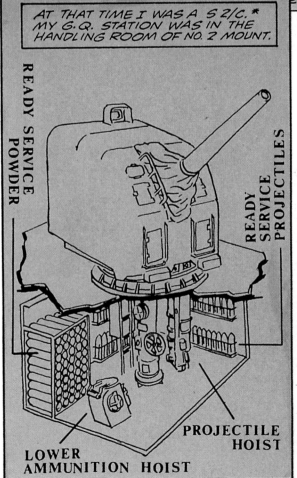

AT THAT TIME I WAS A S 2/C.* MY G.Q. STATION WAS IN THE HANDLING ROOM OF NO. 2 MOUNT.

READY SERVICE POWDER

READY SERVICE PROJECTILES

PROJECTILE HOIST

LOWER AMMUNITION HOIST

PAUL "PINKY" BERKMAN, A BUDDY OF MINE, WAS ALSO IN THE HANDLING ROOM.

WHAT'SA MATTER, SAM, HAVIN' TROUBLE?

NO WONDER THEY CALL US DECK APES! YOU GOTTA BE AN APE TO GET IN HERE! GIMME A HAND, PAUL!

* S 2/C--SEAMAN SECOND CLASS.

14

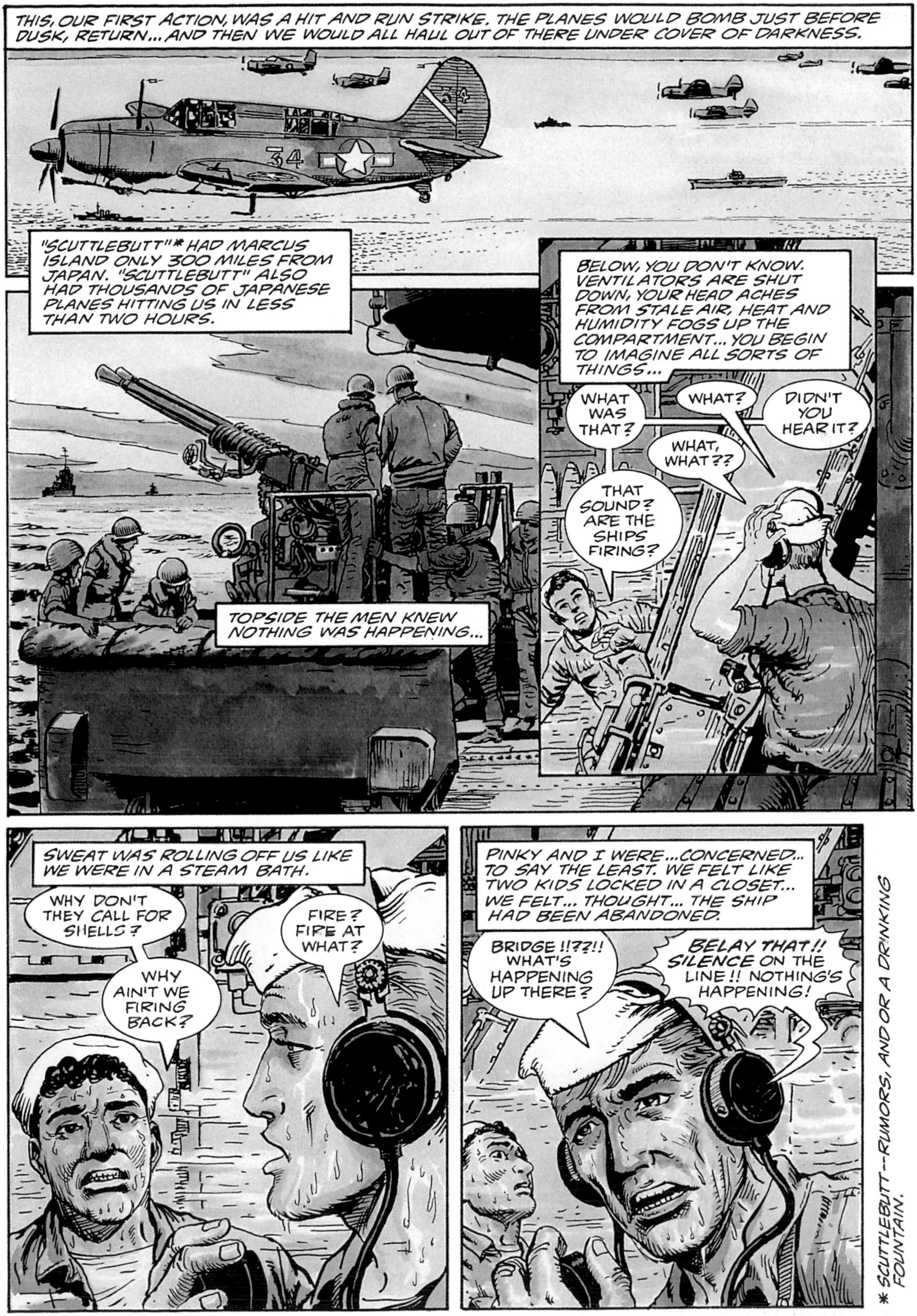
THIS, OUR FIRST ACTION, WAS A HIT AND RUN STRIKE. THE PLANES WOULD BOMB JUST BEFORE DUSK, RETURN... AND THEN WE WOULD ALL HAUL OUT OF THERE UNDER COVER OF DARKNESS.
34
"SCUTTLEBUTT"* HAD MARCUS ISLAND ONLY 300 MILES FROM JAPAN. "SCUTTLEBUTT" ALSO HAD THOUSANDS OF JAPANESE PLANES HITTING US IN LESS THAN TWO HOURS.
TOPSIDE THE MEN KNEW NOTHING WAS HAPPENING...
BELOW, YOU DON'T KNOW. VENTILATORS ARE SHUT DOWN, YOUR HEAD ACHES FROM STALE AIR, HEAT AND HUMIDITY FOGS UP THE COMPARTMENT... YOU BEGIN TO IMAGINE ALL SORTS OF THINGS...
WHAT WAS THAT?
WHAT?
DIDN'T YOU HEAR IT?
WHAT, WHAT??
THAT SOUND? ARE THE SHIPS FIRING?
SWEAT WAS ROLLING OFF US LIKE WE WERE IN A STEAM BATH.
WHY DON'T THEY CALL FOR SHELLS?
WHY AIN'T WE FIRING BACK?
FIRE? FIRE AT WHAT?
PINKY AND I WERE...CONCERNED... TO SAY THE LEAST. WE FELT LIKE TWO KIDS LOCKED IN A CLOSET... WE FELT... THOUGHT... THE SHIP HAD BEEN ABANDONED.
BRIDGE !!??!! WHAT'S HAPPENING UP THERE?
BELAY THAT!! SILENCE ON THE LINE!! NOTHING'S HAPPENING!

* SCUTTLEBUTT--RUMORS, AND OR A DRINKING FOUNTAIN.

NOTHING HAPPENED...ALTHOUGH OUR FIRST ACTION WAS DEEP IN ENEMY WATERS IT WAS A LIMITED RISK OPERATION...PROVIDING VALUABLE TRAINING FOR THE NEW PILOTS AND SHIP'S CREWS. THE PLANES RETURNED AT DUSK PASSING OVER US.

I DON'T KNOW WHY, BUT SUDDENLY THE MOUNT...

CRIPES! THEY'RE CALLIN' FOR A STAR SHELL!

WHAT'S HAPPENIN'? WHAT'S HAPPENIN'?

I DON'T KNOW, GET HOT, SEND THAT SHELL UP, PAUL!

WE SENT IT UP... THEY CALLED FOR ANOTHER...

ULP!!

MAYBE IT WAS THE SWEAT, OR PAUL SLIPPED...

YEEOW!!

MEDIC!! GUN 52... LOWER HANDLING ROOM!

ANOTHER SEAMAN TOOK HIS STATION...

WHAT'S THAT??

WE HELPED PAUL OUT.

IT'S PAUL'S FINGER!! HE FORGOT HIS FINGER!!

16

THAT NIGHT, STANDING AT CONDITION TWO,* AND MAKING FLANK SPEED, WE PUT QUITE A BIT OF DISTANCE BETWEEN US AND MARCUS ISLAND...

THE NEXT DAY WE WERE FAR ASEA AND ALONE. ABOARD SHIP OUR GUNNERS PRACTICED ON THE LOADING MACHINE.*

OFF DUTY CREW MEMBERS WERE DOING... WHAT OFF DUTY CREW MEMBERS DO. "FLY-BOY" WAS CLEANING HIS "POP-GUN".

"PINKY", BUCK AND I WERE SHOOTING THE BREEZE. "PINKY'S" ACCIDENT WAS PAINFUL BUT NO BIG DEAL. THE FIRST JOINT OF HIS LITTLE FINGER WAS MISSING, THAT'S HOW HE GOT THE NAME "PINKY".

I THI...

HEY PINKY! YOU GETTIN' THE PURPLE HEART? I HEAR THEY GIVE EXTRA PAY FOR MEDALS!

EXTRA PAY? YOU IDIOTS! IF YOU GOT THE CONGRESSIONAL MEDAL OF HONOR...YOU KNOW WHAT EXTRA PAY YOU'D GET? TWO BUCKS! WHAT'RE YOU... A SEAMAN SECOND CLASS? HA! MAKIN' 54 BUCKS A MONTH? THAT EXTRA WOULD MEAN 56 BUCKS A MONTH! HA! HA!

* CONDITION TWO—A SURPRISE ATTACK MAY TAKE PLACE AT ANY TIME. THE WATCH IS FOUR HOURS ON AND FOUR OFF.
* LOADING MACHINE—A DUMMY BREECH OF A 5 INCH GUN...STANDARD EQUIPMENT ON DESTROYERS.

17

ON SEPT. 10, 1943 OUR CARRIER T/F* STRUCK AT TARAWA. STILL TO BE PROVEN IN BATTLE THE STEVENS' CREW WAS SHOCKED TO SEE...

BOGIES!

"FLYBOY" HAD BEEN ON A RECONNAISSANCE AND GUNFIRE SPOTTING MISSION. NOW HE WAS HIGH-TAILING IT HOME...

...RETURNING FROM HIS "SIGHT-SEEING TRIP," BRINGING UN-INVITED GUESTS.

THE STEVENS, WITH ITS' CATAPULT, LOOKED LIKE A LIGHT CRUISER TO THE JAPANESE PILOTS... A PRIME TARGET.

IT WASN'T FUNNY. THAT CAT TOOK UP SPACE NORMALLY OCCUPIED BY GUNS AND TORPEDO TUBES. WE MISSED THAT EXTRA FIRE POWER.

* T/F -- TASK FORCE.

18

THEY WERE HIGH ALTITUDE BOMBERS... NOT DIVE BOMBERS. WE KEPT 'EM OFF... BARELY.

THIS WASN'T THE DAY OF THE KAMIKAZE... IN FACT WE HADN'T EVEN HEARD OF 'EM. YET... THESE PLANES DROPPED THEIR BOMBS FROM A SAFE HEIGHT AND LEFT.

WELL, WELL, OUR LITTLE BLUE BIRD HAS COME HOME TO ROOST!

MEBBE WE SHOULD'A SHOT HIM DOWN!

THAT SCOUT PLANE WAS A MONKEY ON OUR BACKS. WE REALLY HATED IT. ABOUT AS MUCH AS "FLYBOY" HATED DESTROYER DUTY.

TARAWA, LIKE MARCUS, WAS A HIT AND RUN RAID. THESE RAIDS CAMOUFLAGED AMERICAN STRATEGIC INTENTIONS. U.S. CARRIER T/F STRIKING HERE AND THERE IN LIGHTNING-LIKE RAIDS...

...PREVENTED JAPAN FROM FINDING OUR PACIFIC FLEET... OR EVEN GUESSING AT ITS NEXT TARGET. AFTER HITTING TARAWA, OUR PLANES RETURNED AND WE SCOOTED OUT OF THERE.

19

"SCUTTLEBUTT" HAD IT WE WOULD BE HITTING GUAM NEXT... AFTER ALL, DIDN'T ONE OR TWO OF OUR OFFICERS APPEAR... APPREHENSIVE??

BUT STRANGE THINGS BEGAN HAPPENING. THE "OLD TIMERS" WERE "DRESSING UP", MAKING BLACKJACKS, PADDLES AND... WHIPS??

A YEOMAN WENT ABOUT PAINTING A LARGE "P" ON CERTAIN CREW MEMBERS, MYSELF INCLUDED.

OFFICERS WERE NOT SPARED. THEIR... APPREHENSION... GREW.

YOU'RE ON MY LIST! ... LT. SIR!!

THE U.S.S. STEVENS DROPPED TO ONE THIRD SPEED.

ALL HANDS!! WE ARE ABOUT TO ENTER THE ROYAL DOMAIN OF KING NEPTUNE...ALL POLLYWOGS BEWARE!

AND THEN WE KNEW... WE WERE CROSSING THE EQUATOR. A NAVY TRADITION WAS ABOUT TO TAKE PLACE.

SHELLBACKS (SEAMEN WHO HAD CROSSED THE EQUATOR BEFORE)...

...IMPOUNDED THE POLLYWOGS (THOSE WHO HAD NOT.)

THE POLLYWOGS WERE PRESENTED TO KING NEPTUNE.

THE GOOD SHIP U.S.S. STEVENS CARRIES A LARGE AND SLIMY CARGO OF LANDLUBBERS, LOUNGE LIZARDS, SAND CRABS, SEA LAWYERS, PLOW DESERTERS, FOUR FLUSHERS, CROSS WORD PUZZLE BUGS, FOUL ROPE INHALERS, LONG BEACH COWBOYS, LIBERTY HOUNDS AND HAY TOSSERS MASQUERADING...

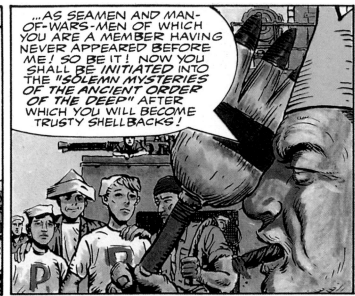

...AS SEAMEN AND MAN-OF-WARS-MEN OF WHICH YOU ARE A MEMBER HAVING NEVER APPEARED BEFORE ME! SO BE IT! NOW YOU SHALL BE INITIATED INTO THE "SOLEMN MYSTERIES OF THE ANCIENT ORDER OF THE DEEP" AFTER WHICH YOU WILL BECOME TRUSTY SHELLBACKS!

FIRST A HAIRCUT, FOLLOWED BY A ROYAL FEAST... OF KITCHEN SLOP.

NEXT A BATH OF BLACK FUEL OIL TO REMOVE ALL TRACES OF BEACH SAND, FLOWER SCENT, AND POLLEN DUST.

POLLYWOG OFFICERS WERE NOT SLIGHTED.

AHA! LT. TUCKER! WELCOME!!

POLLYWOGS WERE HURRIED... AND HARRIED THROUGH A GAUNTLET. FOR ON THIS DAY KING NEPTUNE AND HIS COHORTS RULED SUPREME.

AND SO IT WENT UNTIL...

CEASE ALL FESTIVITIES!! SWEEPERS MAN YOUR BROOMS... CLEAN AND SWEEP DOWN FORE AND AFT... SET CONDITION THREE!

21

THE SCUTTLEBUTT ABOUT GUAM WAS WAY OFF... FOR ON OCTOBER 11, 1943 WE PULLED INTO SAN FRANCISCO BAY.

OUR AIRCRAFT WAS REMOVED... ARMAMENT REPLACED... AND ALL HANDS GRANTED A TWO WEEKS LEAVE.

MOST OF THE MEN WENT HOME TO FAMILIES. I RETURNED TO MY MOUNTAIN HOME AND BEAUTY.

HEY SAM!! SHE KNEW YOU WERE COMING HOME! SHE'S BEEN WAITING AT THE GATE FOR THE PAST THREE DAYS... SHE KNEW!!

YEAH!! YEAH!!

IT WAS WINTER... COLD AND DREARY. BEAUTY HAD LOST SOME WEIGHT AND LOOKED TERRIBLE. BUT IN THOSE TWO WEEKS SHE FILLED OUT AND BECAME HER OLD JOYFUL SELF.

WELL, ALL GOOD THINGS COME TO AN END. ONCE MORE I HAD TO SAY FAREWELL TO BEAUTY AND RETURN TO THE STEVENS. THIS TIME PETE HAD TO TIE BEAUTY UP TO KEEP HER FROM RUNNING AFTER ME.

ARF!! ARF!!

SOMEHOW THE SHIP HAD CAPTURED MY SOUL. I WAS ALMOST HAPPY TO BE BACK... AS WE PUT OUT TO SEA, LITTLE DID I KNOW IT WOULD BE ALMOST TWO YEARS BEFORE WE WOULD RETURN.

ARRIVING AT PEARL, I FOUND IT BURSTING WITH SHIPS OF ALL SORTS... AMERICAN SHIP BUILDERS WERE TURNING THEM OUT IN THE HUNDREDS.

IN OUR ABSENCE BATTLES HAD RAGED BACK AND FORTH... TREMENDOUS BATTLES... OF DEATH AND SUFFERING...

...OF SHIPS AND PLANES...

··· MEN AND TANKS...

... AND OF AMERICAN VICTORIES. THE U.S. WAS NOW ON THE OFFENSIVE.

LATE IN JAN. 1944 WE WERE ASSIGNED TO T/F 58 AND LEFT PEARL FOR THE MARSHALLS. THIS WAS NOT TO BE A HIT AND RUN STRIKE BUT AN INVASION. THE U.S. WAS STEPPING UP ITS OFFENSIVE.

OFF KAWAJALEIN WE BEGAN OUR SHELLING, "SOFTENING UP" THE ISLAND... "MOWING THE LAWN"... CALLED A "SPRUANCE HAIRCUT" NOW.

FOR THREE DAYS AND NIGHTS PLANES AND SHIPS POUNDED THAT ISLAND... UNTIL IT WAS VIRTUALLY STRIPPED CLEAN.

DURING THIS TIME I NOTICED A CHANGE IN BUCK. HE BECAME VERY SECRETIVE.

WHAT'CHA MAKIN', BUCK?

A LOT OF SEAMEN CARRIED HANDMADE KNIVES...

YOU'LL SEE, LADDIE!

BUCK WAS MAKING ONE... IT WAS TREMENDOUS.

?

I'M GOING HOME!!

WHEN OUR FIRE SUPPORT WAS NO LONGER NEEDED AT KWAJALEIN WE PULLED CLEAR. UNDERWAY FOR FUNAFUTI WE RESUMED NORMAL SHIPS ROUTINE... POSTED DAILY IT RAN SOMEWHAT LIKE THIS...

0600   CALL CMAA, MAA OF MESS HALL, AND STEWARD.

0625   CALL REVEILLE P.O.'S.

0630   REVEILLE. UP ALL HANDS TRICE UP ALL BUNKS.

PINKY, I'M GETTIN' FED UP WITH ALL THIS TURN TO STUFF! ALL THIS CHIPPIN' AN' PAINTIN' AIN'T GETTIN' ME NOWHERE!

WHAT'CHA GONNA DO ABOUT IT, SAM?

0700   BREAKFAST.

0800   TURN TO COMMENCE ROUTINE SHIP'S WORK.

1130   DINNER.

I'M GONNA BE A SNIPE!

REMEMBER THEM SNIPES TELLIN' US THEY DON'T HAVE TO TURN TO? WELL I'M STRIKING* FOR A RATE! I'M GONNA BE A SNIPE!

1300   TURN TO CONTINUE SHIP'S WORK.

1700   SUPPER.

1800   DARKEN SHIP SMOKING LAMP IS OUT.

HEY PINKY!! I GOT THE O.K.! I'M TO REPORT TO CHIEF WIPPIT IN THE AFT ENGINE ROOM TOMORROW!

* STRIKE, STRIKER -- A NON-RATED MAN WORKING TO QUALIFY FOR A PETTY-OFFICER'S RATE.

THE NEXT MORNING...

CHIEF WIPPIT?

YESSIR!

OKAY STRIKER! GET A WIRE BRUSH, SOME OIL AN' A RAG...START WIRE BRUSHING THESE DECK PLATES! TURN TO!!

YEAH! YOU THE STRIKER? GLANZMAN, S 2/C?

TURN TO? RIGHT THEN I KNEW I HAD MADE A MISTAKE. THIS WAS THE ENGINE ROOM, I WAS STRIKING FOR AN ENGINEER'S RATE.

THOSE SNIPES I HAD TALKED TO WERE FIREMEN IN THE FIREROOM. I SHOULD HAVE STRUCK FOR A FIREMAN'S RATE.

NEXT, THE CHIEF HANDED ME A CHECK LIST...I HAD TO CRAWL IN THE BILGES TO TAKE READINGS ON ALL SORTS OF GAUGES...IT GAVE ME AN IDEA.

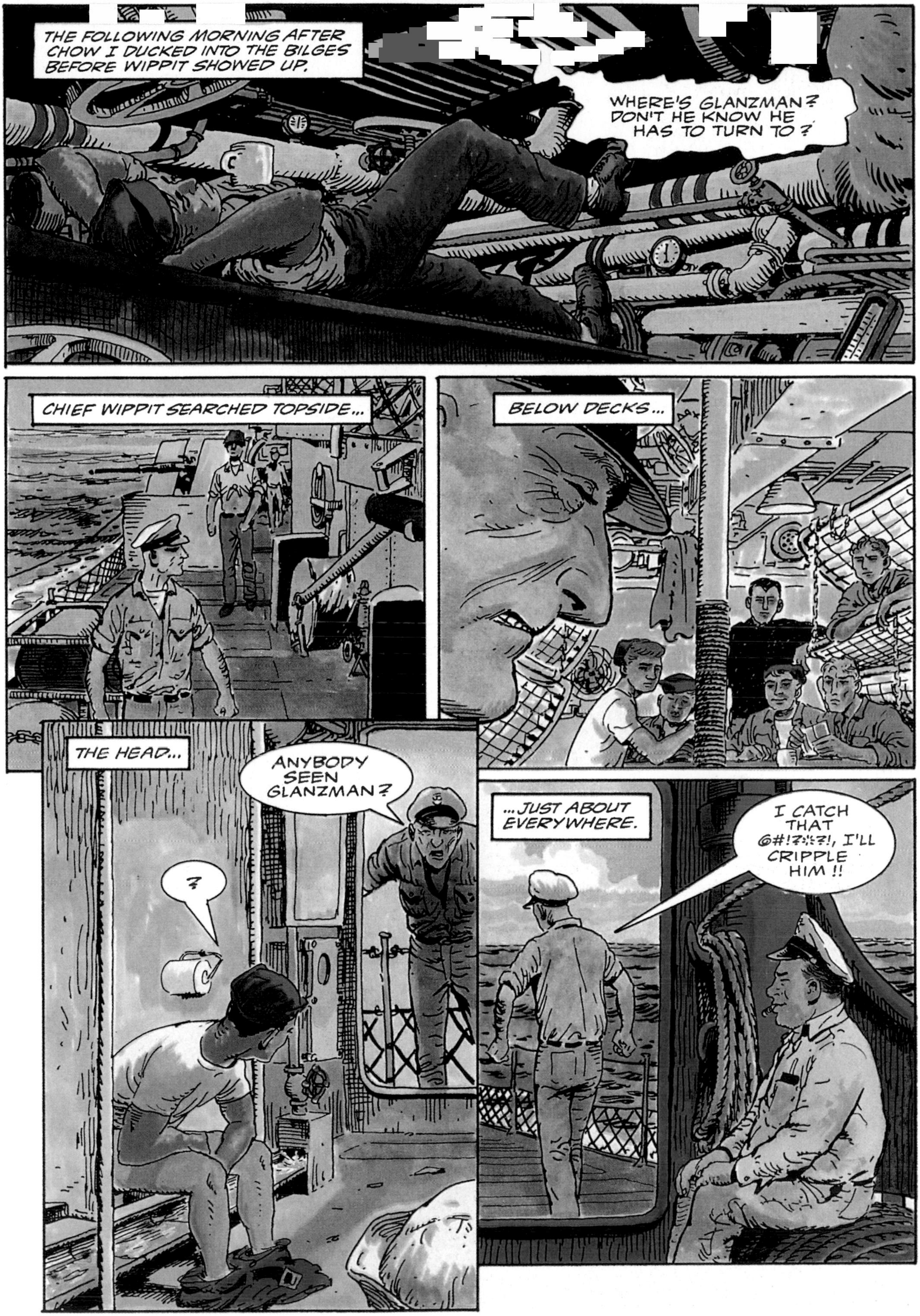
THE FOLLOWING MORNING AFTER CHOW I DUCKED INTO THE BILGES BEFORE WIPPIT SHOWED UP.
WHERE'S GLANZMAN? DON'T HE KNOW HE HAS TO TURN TO?
CHIEF WIPPIT SEARCHED TOPSIDE...
BELOW DECKS...
THE HEAD...
ANYBODY SEEN GLANZMAN?
?
...JUST ABOUT EVERYWHERE.
I CATCH THAT @#!?*?!, I'LL CRIPPLE HIM!!

OF COURSE I HAD TO GO ON WATCH...AN' THAT'S WHEN WIPPIT CAUGHT ME. THE BALLOON'S BLANK 'CAUSE I CAN'T REPEAT WHAT HE SAID...BUT IT WASN'T GOOD.

WELL...I KIND'A GOT MAD. SO I KEPT HIDIN' ON HIM...

ANYBODY SEEN GLANZMAN?

...SOMETIMES I HID BETWEEN THE SACKS THAT WERE TRICED UP...

...SOMETIMES IN A HANDLING ROOM...

...OR UP ON A STACK.

IT GOT TO BE A GAME WITH ME...BUT CHIEF WIPPIT WAS FIT TO BE TIED. EVERY WATCH HE'D CATCH ME...AND BLOW UP. YET, HE *NEVER* PUT ME ON REPORT! (HE WASN'T SUCH A BAD GUY.)

MOLSKY, THE FIREROOM CHIEF, THOUGHT IT WAS A BIG JOKE.

I'LL FIND HIM!

HAW! HAW!!

I BEEN TRYING TO GET BACK AT THAT OLD GEEZER EVER SINCE HE... WELL, THAT'S PERSONAL. BUT YOU... BOY! YOU'RE DOING ONE HELL OF A JOB ON HIM!

YEAH! BUT ONE DAY HE'S GONNA PUNCH ME BLIND OR ELSE PUT ME ON REPORT!!

WHY DON'T YOU STRIKE FOR FIREMAN? I'LL TALK TO WIPPIT... GET HIM TO TRANSFER YOU.

COME DOWN INTO THE FIREROOM WITH ME, I'LL TAKE GOOD CARE OF YOU.

?

"COME DOWN INTO THE FIREROOM WITH ME"...I WASN'T SO SURE I LIKED THE WAY MOLSKY SAID THAT. BUT HE WAS ALWAYS KIDDING AROUND...I FIGURED IT WAS O.K.

ANYBODY SEEN THAT G#☆!?! GLANZMAN?

...MEANWHILE I KEPT CLEAR OF WIPPIT.

29

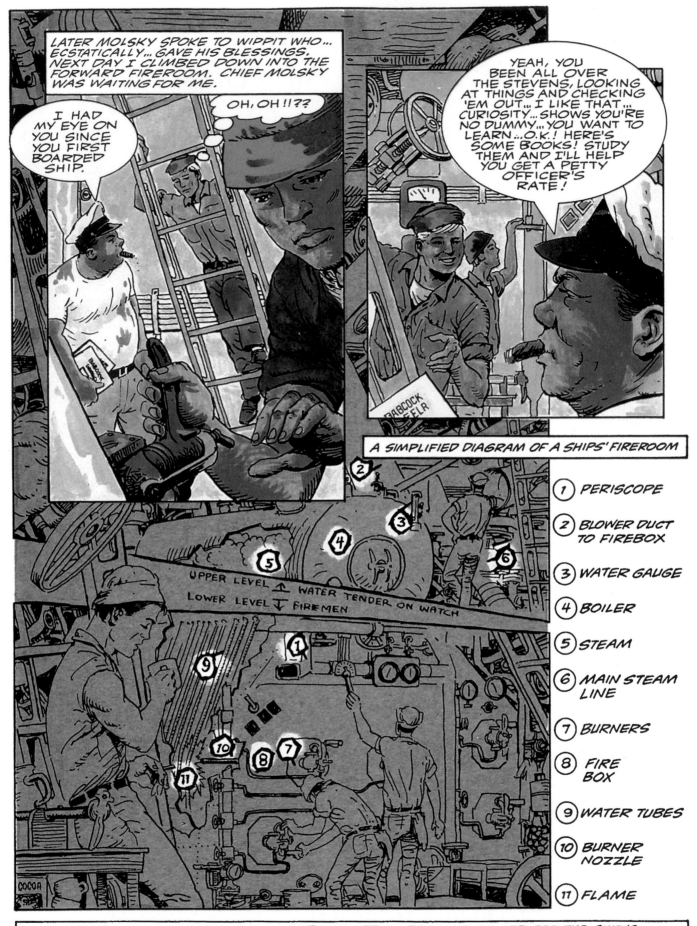

A SIMPLIFIED DIAGRAM OF A SHIPS' FIREROOM

① PERISCOPE

② BLOWER DUCT TO FIREBOX

③ WATER GAUGE

④ BOILER

⑤ STEAM

⑥ MAIN STEAM LINE

⑦ BURNERS

⑧ FIRE BOX

⑨ WATER TUBES

⑩ BURNER NOZZLE

⑪ FLAME

THE FIREROOMS ARE WHERE STEAM IS PRODUCED TO PROVIDE POWER FOR THE SHIP'S TURBINES, SORT OF LIKE A HUGE FURNACE. WHEN THE SHIP IS MANEUVERING FIREMEN MUST "PUNCH" OR "PULL" BURNERS TO KEEP THE STEAM PRESSURE CONSTANT... SIMULTANEOUSLY WATERTENDERS MUST OPEN OR CLOSE VALVES TO MAINTAIN PROPER WATER LEVEL IN THE BOILERS.

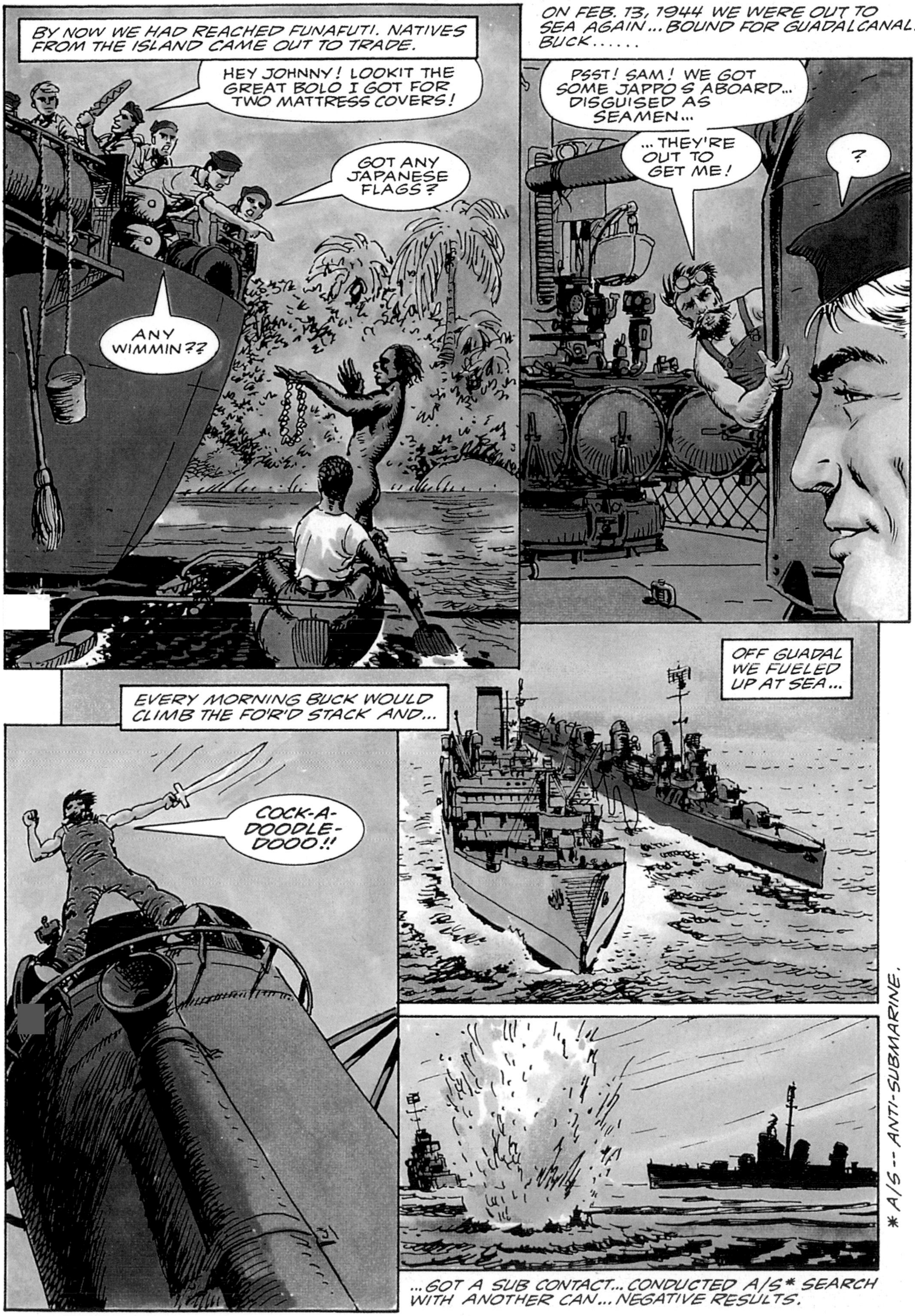
BY NOW WE HAD REACHED FUNAFUTI. NATIVES FROM THE ISLAND CAME OUT TO TRADE.
HEY JOHNNY! LOOKIT THE GREAT BOLO I GOT FOR TWO MATTRESS COVERS!
GOT ANY JAPANESE FLAGS?
ANY WIMMIN??
ON FEB. 13, 1944 WE WERE OUT TO SEA AGAIN... BOUND FOR GUADALCANAL. BUCK......
PSST! SAM! WE GOT SOME JAPPO S ABOARD... DISGUISED AS SEAMEN...
... THEY'RE OUT TO GET ME!
?
EVERY MORNING BUCK WOULD CLIMB THE FO'R'D STACK AND...
COCK-A-DOODLE-DOOO!!
OFF GUADAL WE FUELED UP AT SEA...
...GOT A SUB CONTACT... CONDUCTED A/S* SEARCH WITH ANOTHER CAN... NEGATIVE RESULTS.
* A/S -- ANTI-SUBMARINE.

ABOUT THIS TIME BUCK REALLY WENT OFF THE DEEP END... HE ACCUSED ME OF INCITING A MUTINY.

AHA!! FIREARMS IS IT? FOR YOUR MUTINIOUS PLANS NO DOUBT!

FIREARMS? YOU KIDDIN', BUCK? THIS IS SOME LEFT OVER CAKE I'M TAKIN' BELOW!

HE WAS ALL OVER THAT SHIP...LOOKING FOR THEM "DISGUISED" JAPANESE.

AHA! I SEE YOU! BY GAWD YE'LL NOT ESCAPE ME THIS TIME!

BUCK HAD BEEN IN THE NAVY 8 YEARS...AT PEARL ON DEC. 7, 1941... TRAPPED IN THE CAPSIZED OKLA-HOMA FOR 14 HOURS...WHEN THE RESCUE PARTY CUT THROUGH THE HULL HE CAME OUT SCREAMING... BUCK HAD HAD IT...

...AND THE SKIPPER ALMOST HAD IT...

AGGGGAAHH!

BUCK TRIED TO LOP HIS HEAD OFF WITH THAT "KNIFE" HE HAD...WE ALL JUMPED BUCK... TIED HIM UP AN'...

BUCK WAS TRANSFERRED TO A HOSPITAL SHIP... RECEIVED A MEDICAL DISCHARGE AND WENT HOME...

...WELL, BUCK SAID HE WAS GOING HOME!

OF COURSE WE HAD OUR SHARE OF ATTACKING PLANES, BUT ONCE A LONE BETTY CAME SKIMMING IN LOW, SCOOTING BETWEEN THE SHIPS...

...WE COULDN'T FIRE FOR FEAR OF HITTING NEARBY SHIPS...

...AND, AGAIN ONCE... SINCE WE HADN'T HAD LIBERTY IN QUITE A FEW MONTHS THE SKIPPER DECIDED TO DO SOMETHING ABOUT IT.

LIBERTY PARTY LAY UP TO THE QUARTER-DECK FOR LIBERTY!

...I DON'T KNOW WHAT HE WAS UP TO...HE JUST CAME IN AND LEFT.

OUR SHIP (I DON'T KNOW ABOUT OTHERS) CARRIED BEER ABOARD... BUT SINCE THE U.S.N. FORBADE DRINKING ON BOARD...

...WE HAD TO LAY OFF THE SHIP AND DRINK OUR BEER, RETURNING, ANOTHER "LIBERTY" SECTION WENT OUT.... BACK AND FORTH THE M.W.B.* WENT UNTIL ALL LIBERTY SECTIONS HAD "LIBERTY."

* M.W.B. -- MOTOR WHALE BOAT

LATE FEBUARY OR EARLY MARCH WE WERE BOMBARDING NUSA AND NUSALIK ISLANDS OFF KAVEING, NEW IRELAND.

APRIL WE SCREENED LCT'S AND LCI'S TAKING PART IN THE LANDINGS AT HOLLANDIA, NEW GUINEA... HERE OUR MAIL CAUGHT UP TO US. A LETTER FROM PETE WAS ABOUT BEAUTY... IT DIDN'T SOUND TOO GOOD.

and I can't keep Beauty tied up, she howls something terrible. She's back over at your place, waiting at the gate. I been taking her food to her. She won't leave that spot. Otherwise, ...

HEY! AIN'T WE BEEN HERE BEFORE?

MAY AND JUNE WE DID CONVOY DUTY, HUMBOLT BAY, TULAGI, KAWAJALEIN, BACK AND FORTH, AGAIN AND AGAIN.

AROUND THE MIDDLE OF JUNE T/F 58 STRUCK SAIPAN. SOME DD'S,* SEAPLANES AND SUBMARINES WERE STATIONED OFF TARGETS UNDERGOING ATTACK.

THIS WAS A U.S. POLICY... IT GUARANTEED A HIGH PERCENTAGE OF DOWNED PILOTS BEING RESCUED.

ONE PILOT, HIS AVENGER DAMAGED BY FLAK OVER SAIPAN, WAS FORCED "INTO THE DRINK."

HE WAS RESCUED AND RETURNED TO HIS CARRIER, THE ENTERPRISE. THIS RESCUED PILOT, COMMANDER BILL MARTIN, LATER BECAME COMMANDER OF THE SIXTH FLEET.

* DD'S -- DESTROYERS

AROUND THIS TIME WE HAD ANOTHER SO-CALLED "LIBERTY."

LIBERTY PARTY LAY UP TO THE QUARTERDECK!

THIS TIME I DIDN'T BOTHER WITH A CLEAN SHIRT AN' HAT.

HEY! LOOKIT! AN ISLAND!

GREAT, THERE OUGHTTA BE SOME WIMMIN ON IT!

AT LEAST WE CAN DRINK OUR WARM BEER ON LAND!

BUT A CORAL REEF PREVENTED US FROM BEACHING THE BOAT.

WHAT'A WE GONNA DO?

WHAT'D YOU THINK BABY!

SWIM FOR IT!

SUPPOSE YOU CAN'T SWIM?

WE'LL LEAVE YOU A BOTTLE! HA! HA!

I COULDN'T SWIM...

WASN'T ANYTHING ON THAT TWO-BIT ISLAND ANYWAY... 'FACT IT WAS SO SMALL YOU COULD SPIT ACROSS IT. WOMEN?? THERE WASN'T EVEN BIRDS ON IT.

36

AFTER SAIPAN, SOMETIME IN JULY WE HIT GUAM. BY THIS TIME I HAD MADE FIREMAN GRADE FIRST CLASS AND EARNING 66 BUCKS A MONTH. MY G.Q. STATION WAS THEN IN THE FIREROOM.

...BELOW DECKS WE HEARD THE BATTLE RAGING ABOVE US

WE'RE O-K, AS LONG AS THE FIVE INCHERS ARE FIRING!

OH! OH! THEY'RE GETTIN' CLOSE! THE 40s AND 20s ARE OPENIN' UP!

WE HAD BEEN IN A FEW SCRAPS BEFORE... SHOT DOWN MAYBE FIVE PLANES AND BY THE SOUNDS TOPSIDE WE KNEW WHAT WAS HAPPENING...

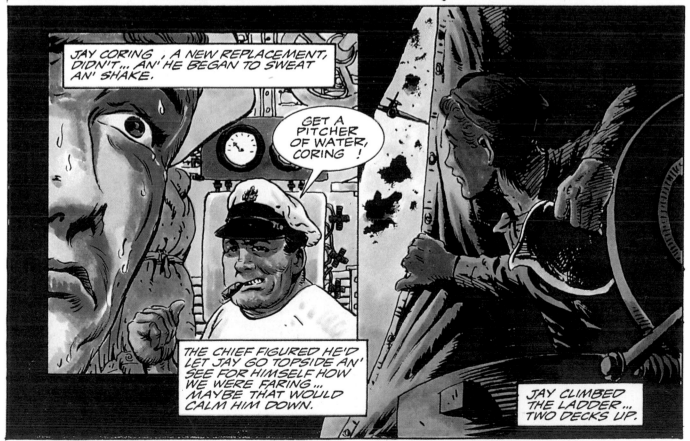

JAY CORING , A NEW REPLACEMENT, DIDN'T... AN' HE BEGAN TO SWEAT AN' SHAKE.

GET A PITCHER OF WATER, CORING !

THE CHIEF FIGURED HE'D LET JAY GO TOPSIDE AN' SEE FOR HIMSELF HOW WE WERE FARING ... MAYBE THAT WOULD CALM HIM DOWN.

JAY CLIMBED THE LADDER ... TWO DECKS UP.

SQUIRMING PAST THE CANVAS LIGHT BAFFLE JAY WAS TEMPORARILY BLINDED BY THE BRIGHT SUNLIGHT... HE NEVER REACHED THE SCUTTLEBUTT.

A WALL OF HEAT AND SOUND CRASHED AGAINST HIM... CORDITE AND SMOKING SHELL CASES STUNG HIS NOSTRILS... CORK, DUST AND CHIPS OF PAINT WERE FLYING IN THE AIR... THE STEVENS WAS THROBBING, THRASHING, TWISTING, TURNING AND ASHAKEN'...

JAY CORING DOVE BACK DOWN INTO THE FIREROOM... NEVER MIND THE LADDER...

HE WANTED TO RUN, HIDE, COVER HIMSELF, DISAPPEAR... HE SHUT HIS EYES AND WEPT. WE DID NOT PITY OR DESPISE HIM. HE WAS JUST THERE... SOMETHING... THERE. AND WE WERE TOO BUSY TO THINK OF HIM... GUAM WAS BEING POUNDED.

CLIMAXING SEVENTEEN DAYS OF UNPARALLELLED AERIAL AND SURFACE BOMBARDMENT THE INVASION GOT UNDERWAY JULY 20 1944.

DURING A LULL I WENT TOPSIDE... MARINE CASUALTIES WERE BEING BROUGHT OFF THE BEACHES... A STEADY STREAM OF BOATS... ONE AFTER THE OTHER... SWEPT PAST OUR BOW HEADING FOR THE HOSPITAL SHIP.

GUAM WAS NOT SECURED UNTIL AUG. 10 AND IN THAT TWO MONTH CAMPAIGN JAPAN LOST 1,223 AIRCRAFT.

THE COMMANDING GENERAL OF THE THIRD MARINE DIVISION PRESENTED THE STEVENS WITH A COMMENDATION FOR ITS EXPERT MARKSMANSHIP AND FIRE SUPPORT.

...THE STEVENS CREW LINED UP FOR CHOW.

LEAVING THE AREA THE STEVENS ESCORTED UNITS OF T/F 77 PROCEEDING FROM AITAPE TO MOROTAI... HERE WE HAD PATROL DUTY.

?

FIVE!

EVERY NOW AND THEN A SWABBIE WOULD STOP AT THE SICK BAY...

SIX!

NINE DAYS LATER WE ESCORTED SOME TRANSPORTS TO NEW GUINEA.

?

THREE!

I SAW SOME MONEY PASS HANDS.

FROM THERE... AGAIN BACK TO MOROTAI WITH A RE-INFORCEMENT ECHELON.

I WAS CURIOUS. I STUCK MY HEAD INTO "DOC'S" "OFFICE."

SEVEN!

SEVEN WAS MY LUCKY NUMBER, WHAT DID I HAVE TO LOSE??

SEVEN BUCKS!

WHAT?

SEVEN BUCKS! YOU OWE ME SEVEN BUCKS, SAM!

PhM* "DOC" ARNOLD HAD A PILE OF CIGARETTE PAPERS AN' A SCALPEL IN FRONT OF HIM. SEVEN PIECES WERE NEATLY CUT THROUGH, THE EIGHTH ON DOWN WASN'T TOUCHED ...GIVE HIM A NUMBER... IF HE CUT THROUGH MORE OR LESS HE OWED YOU, OTHERWISE YOU OWED HIM.

* PhM -- PHARMACISTS MATE.

40

AIRCRAFT SWEPT IN TO ATTACK THE MOROTAI RE-INFORCEMENT GROUP WHILE THE STEVENS WAS ON PICKET DUTY.

LATER JOINING TASK GROUP 78.6 WHILE SCREENING RE-INFORCEMENTS FROM HOLLANDIA TO MINDORO...

...THE STEVENS WAS CALLED OUT TO GIVE ASSISTANCE TO U.S.S. SHELTON, A DESTROYER ESCORT THAT HAD BEEN TORPEDOED.

WE REACHED HER WITHIN HOURS. ANOTHER DE-STROYER, THE ROWELL, HAD ALREADY TAKEN OFF THE SHELTON'S CREW.

THE SHELTON'S TORN REAR PROTRUDED AT AN OBSCENE ANGLE... HER BOILER AND ENGINE ROOMS WERE FLOODED, HER STEERING GEAR SHATTERED... SHE LAY ON HER SIDE LISTING LIKE A SICK ANIMAL...

A LIGHT RAIN BEGAN TO FALL AS A THIRD DESTROYER, THE LANG, TOOK HER IN TOW.

WITH THE STEVENS SCREENING, THE LONG TREK TO PORT WAS BEGUN.

...BUT WHILE UNDER TOW THE DAMAGED VESSEL CAPSIZED...

HEAVE IN ALL TOW LINES... SECURE FROM SALVAGE OPERATIONS... GUN CREWS STAND BY TO SINK HER!

42

AT ABOUT 2200 THE PROUD SHIP AWAITED HER DEATH BLOW.

THE RAIN CEASED... MOMENTARILY... AS THOUGH HOLDING ITS' BREATH.

ABOARD THE ROWELL, THE SHELTON'S CREW, HORRIFIED AND HELPLESS, WATCHED HER ASSASSINATION.

TO THOSE CREWMEN, AS WITH ALL TRUE SAILORS, A SHIP IS NOT STEEL AND IRON... BUT A LIVING ENTITY. THEY WOULD ALWAYS REMEMBER HER GREY SHAPE, HER POWERFUL GRACE, THE SURGE OF HER MIGHTY ENGINES AS SHE LUNGED TO THE FOE... AND TOO, THE ALMOST HEAVENLY PEACE AS ON MOON LIT WATERS SHE SEEMED TO GLIDE SILENTLY, STEALTHILY, LEAVING BEHIND A WHITE VEIL IN THE BLACK WATERS. HER WAKE, A PHOSPHORIC WHITE RIBBON WITH FLECKS OF DIAMONDS.

...NOTHING... NO MARKER FOR HER FINAL RESTING PLACE. QUIETLY, LIKE A FUNERAL PROCESSION, THE SHIPS LEFT. COLD DEPRESSING RAIN FELL GENTLY.

TAKEN FROM SKETCHES MADE AT THE TIME.

44

WHILE THE MINDORO INVASION WAS GOING FORWARD HALSEY'S THIRD FLEET WAS PREPARING AN AIR STRIKE IN THE MANILA AREA. HIS DESTROYERS WERE FUELING ON DEC. 17TH 1944.

FUELING OPERATIONS WERE SUSPENDED WHEN A MONSTER TYPHOON TORE INTO THE SHIPS.

ABOARD THE STEVENS THE STARBOARD ANCHOR WAS RIPPED OUT OF THE HAWSE PIPE...FLUNG ABOUT LIKE A STRAW IN THE 80-KNOT WINDS.

WE CAME THROUGH SAFE WITH JUST A BUCKLED BOW.

BUT THE U.S.S. HULL, DRIVEN DOWN BY THE WIND AND 60-FOOT SEAS WAS SWAMPED BY AN AVALANCE OF WATER... 62 MEN SURVIVED.

THE U.S.S. MONAGHAN ALSO WENT DOWN...ONLY 6 MEN SURVIVED. AND THE U.S.S. SPENCE, THE FIRST TO GO DOWN HAD ONLY 23 SURVIVORS.

THESE DESTROYERS WERE EACH MANNED BY ABOUT 320 MEN AND OFFICERS.

IT WOULD REQUIRE ANOTHER 60 PAGES TO DESCRIBE THE ENDLESS DAWN
AND DUSK ALERTS, THE COUNTLESS DAYS OF SHORE BOMBARDMENTS, SUP-
PORT LANDINGS AND CONVOY DUTY . . . MOST OF WHICH WERE CONDUCTED
UNDER ENEMY AIR ATTACK . . . COMBAT IS VIOLENT AND DEATH IN COMBAT
IS HORRIFYING . . . THERE ARE NO WORDS THAT CAN TRULY PORTRAY THIS
EXPERIENCE. FOR THESE REASONS I HAVE OMITTED SUCH TALES . . . .

IN HONOR OF

DESTROYERS AND DESTROYER-ESCORTS AT OKINAWA

(MARCH 26-JUNE 21, 1945.)

Destroyers

AMMEN	GREGORY	PAUL HAMILTON
ANTHONY	GUEST	PICKING
AULICK	HALL	PORTERFIELD
BACHE	HARRY E. HUBBARD	PRESTON
BEALE	HART	PRICHETT
BENNETT	HERNDON	PRINGLE
BENNION	HEYWOOD L. EDWARDS	PURDY
BOYD	HOWORTH	PUTNAM
BRADFORD	HUDSON	RALPH TALBOT
BRAINE	HUGH W. HADLEY	ROOKS
BROWN	HUTCHINS	ROWE
BRYANT	HYMAN	RUSSELL
BUSH	INGERSOLL	SHUBRICK
CAPERTON	INGRAHAM	SMALLEY
CASSIN YOUNG	IRWIN	SPROSTON
CHARLES AUSBURNE	ISHERWOOD	STACK
CHARLES J. BADGER	KIMBERLY	STANLY
CLAXTON	KNAPP	STERETT
COGSWELL	LAFFEY	STODDARD
COLHOUN	LANG	STORMES
COMPTON	LANSDOWNE	THATCHER
CONVERSE	LAWS	TWIGGS
COWELL	LITTLE	VAN VALKENBURGH
DALY	LOWRY	WADSWORTH
DOUGLAS H. FOX	LUCE	WALKE
DREXLER	MANNERT L. ABELE	WATTS
DYSON	MASSEY	WICKES
EVANS	METCALF	WILKES
FARENHOLT	MOALE	WILLARD KEITH
FULLAM	MORRIS	WILSON
FOOTE	MORRISON	WM. D. PORTER
GAINARD	MUSTIN	WREN

Destroyer-Escorts

ABERCROMBIE	GENDREAU	RIDDLE
BEBAS	GILLIGAN	SAMUEL S. MILES
BOWERS	GRADY	SEDERSTROM
BRIGHT	GRISWOLD	SEID
CARLSON	HALLORAN	SNYDER
CONNOLLY	HEMMINGER	STERN
CROSS	HENRY A. WILEY	SWEARER
CROUTER	LA PRADE	TILLS
D.M. CUMMINGS	LERAY WILSON	TISDALE
EDMONDS	MANLOVE	VAMMEN
EISELE	MCCLELLAND	WALTER C. WANN
ENGLAND	METIVIER	WESSON
FAIR	OBERRENDER	WHITEHURST
FIEBERLING	O'NEILL	WILLMARTH
FINNEGAN	PAUL G. BAKER	WITTER
FLEMING	RALL	WM. C. COLE
FOREMAN	R. W. SUESENS	WM. SEIVERLING

 LOST

DESTROYERS AND

Ship	Casualties Killed	Wounded
KIMBERLY (DD)	4	57
PORTERFIELD (DD)	—	1
MURRAY (DD)	1	4
O'BRIEN (DD)	50	76
FOREMAN (DE)	—	1
FRANKS (DD)	—	2
PRICHETT (DD)	2	1
NEWCOMB (DD)	40	51
LEUTZE (DD)	8	30
MULLANY (DD)	30	36
HOWORTH (DD)	9	14
HYMAN (DD)	11	41
MORRIS (DD)	12	45
HARRISON (DD)	—	—
HAYNSWORTH (DD)	12	27
FIEBERLING (DE)	—	—
WESSON (DE)	8	25
BENNETT (DD)	3	18
GREGORY (DD)	—	2

...... SUFFICE TO SAY THE STEVENS HAD HER FAIR SHARE. YET WE WERE FORTUNATE ... PERHAPS BLESSED ... IN THAT WE WERE NOT CALLED INTO THE TERROR OF OKINAWA. AT THE TIME, OKINAWA WAS A DREADED WORD ... IT SEEMED WE WOULD ONLY WHISPER THE WORD IN FEAR; AS IF SOMEHOW THE GODS OF WAR WOULD HEAR AND PERHAPS HURL US INTO THAT HOLOCAUST WHERE SHIPS AND MEN LITERALLY BLED TO DEATH.

THOSE THAT SERVED

DESTROYER- ESCORTS DAMAGED AT OKINAWA *(ABBREVIATED LIST)*

Ship	Casualties Killed	Wounded	Ship	Casualties Killed	Wounded
CHARLES J. BADGER (DD)	—	—	ISHERWOOD (DD)	42	41
MANLOVE (DE)	1	10	HUTCHINS (DD)	1	21
KIDD (DD)	38	55	RALPH TALBOT (DD)	5	9
HANK (DD)	3	1	DALY (DD)	3	33
HALE (DD)	—	2	TWIGGS (DD)	No data	
WHITEHURST (DE)	37	37	HAGGARD (DD)	11	40
BENNION (DD)	1	6	HAZLEWOOD (DD)	46	26
STANLY (DD)	—	3	HUDSON (DD)	—	1
RIDDLE (DE)	1	9	ENGLAND (DE)	34	30
CASSIN YOUNG (DD)	1	59	EVANS (DD)	31	29
RALL (DE)	21	38	HUGH W. HADLEY (DD)	28	67
PURDY (DD)	13	58	BACHE (DD)	41	32
SIGSBEE (DD)	3	75	JOHN C. BUTLER (DE)	—	3
McDERMUT (DD)	2	33	DOUGLAS H. FOX (DD)	9	35
LAFFEY (DD)	32	71	COWELL (DD)	—	2
BOWERS (DE)	48	59	STORMES (DD)	21	16
BRYANT (DD)	34	33	ANTHONY (DD)	—	5
WADSWORTH (DD)	—	1	BRAINE (DD)	50	78
AMMEN (DD)	—	8	SHUBRICK (DD)	32	28

ON THE ROAD TO MANILA ... WE HAD EVERY TYPE OF DUTY IMAGINABLE. AS ESCORT, SCREENING SHIP, RESCUE VESSEL, SCOUT, AND AS PICKET. WE PROVIDED FIRE SUPPORT FOR AMPHIBIOUS LANDINGS, CONDUCTED SHORE BOMBARDMENTS, FOUGHT SUBS, PLANES, PENETRATED ENEMY MINE FIELDS AND HARBORS ... AN' A FEW I'VE FORGOTTEN.

DATES AND PLACES DURING THIS TIME HAVE REALLY ESCAPED MY MIND. LISTED BELOW ARE A FEW THAT COME TO ME ...

MINDORO
LEYTE
LUZON
MANUS IS.
LINGAYEN GULF
TINGANEN PANAY
ILOILO PANAN
SUBIC BAY
MORO GULF
PARANG-MALBANG
LALAYANG POINT
COTABATO
TAMONTACO
SANTA CRUZ
TALOMOC BAY
BRUNEI BAY
NORTH BORNEO
BALIKPAPAN
EAST BORNEO
BUCKNER BAY
OKINAWA
TSINGTAO
CHINA
JINSEN
KOREA

OF COURSE THERE WERE PERIODS OF RELATIVE PEACE WHEN WE WEREN'T AT SEA. WORKING PARTIES MADE UP OF DECK HANDS ...

... WOULD LEAVE THE SHIP AND BRING BACK AMMO AND OR STORES FROM AN ISLAND DEPOT. ESPIRITU SANTO IN THE HEBRIDES WAS ONE SUCH SUPPLY BASE. .

WHAT'CHA GOT?

CANNED SPINICH! ROSSO'S GOT THE GOODIES!

... A CASE OR TWO OF GRAPEFRUIT JUICE OR COCOA WOULD ALWAYS "FIND IT'S WAY" INTO THE FIREROOM ...

HIDE IT QUICK! I THINK BOS'N SMITH SPOTTED US!

ON RARE OCCASIONS SNIPES WERE "PRESSED" INTO THE WORK DETAIL ... AND IF SO ...

AT THESE TIMES A FIRE-ROOM MAY HAVE BEEN SECURED. MANHOLE COVERS REMOVED AND SNIPES WOULD ENTER THE FIREBOXES TO SCRAPE, AND CLEAN THE TUBES. (SEE SKETCH PG. 30.)

OTHER SNIPES WOULD CRAWL INTO BOILERS TO WIRE BRUSH AND CLEAN THEM... IT WAS *HOT* AND DIRTY WORK.

IT WAS A GOOD TIME TO INSPECT AND SERVICE BLOWERS AND AUX. PUMPS ...BILGES WERE PUMPED AND CLEANED.

WE ALSO CRAWLED OVER DUST ENCRUSTED STEAM LINES AND DUCTS. CLEANING AND PAINT-ING... YESSIR! IT WAS *HOT* AND DIRTY WORK.

VISITS TO OTHER SHIPS WERE PERMITTED. THE FIRST TIME I VISITED A CARRIER I WAS DUMBFOUNDED...

HOLY SMOKES! A SODA FOUNTAIN!

ICE CREAM AN' ICE CREAM SODAS! A MIRACLE!

...OUR SHIP HAD NO SUCH NICETIES.

THOSE LARGER SHIPS EVEN HAD A LAUNDRY ROOM AND A *BARBER SHOP!*

OUR HAIR WAS CUT BY "OX", A YEOMAN. HE WOULD SET UP SHOP IN THE AFT 40mm AMMO ROOM. THIS WAS ALSO WHERE OUR MAIL WAS SORTED (WHEN WE GOT IT.)

FUELING FROM A TANKER IN PORT WAS A HECK OF A LOT EASIER THAN AT SEA.... WE WOULD ALSO TRADE MOVIES AND COLLECT OUR MAIL (IF IT CAUGHT UP TO US.)

...MOVIES WERE SHOWN IN THE MESS HALL.

AND ALTHOUGH GAMBLING WAS FORBIDDEN ABOARD SHIP, POKER GAMES ALWAYS FLOURISHED IN PORT.

50

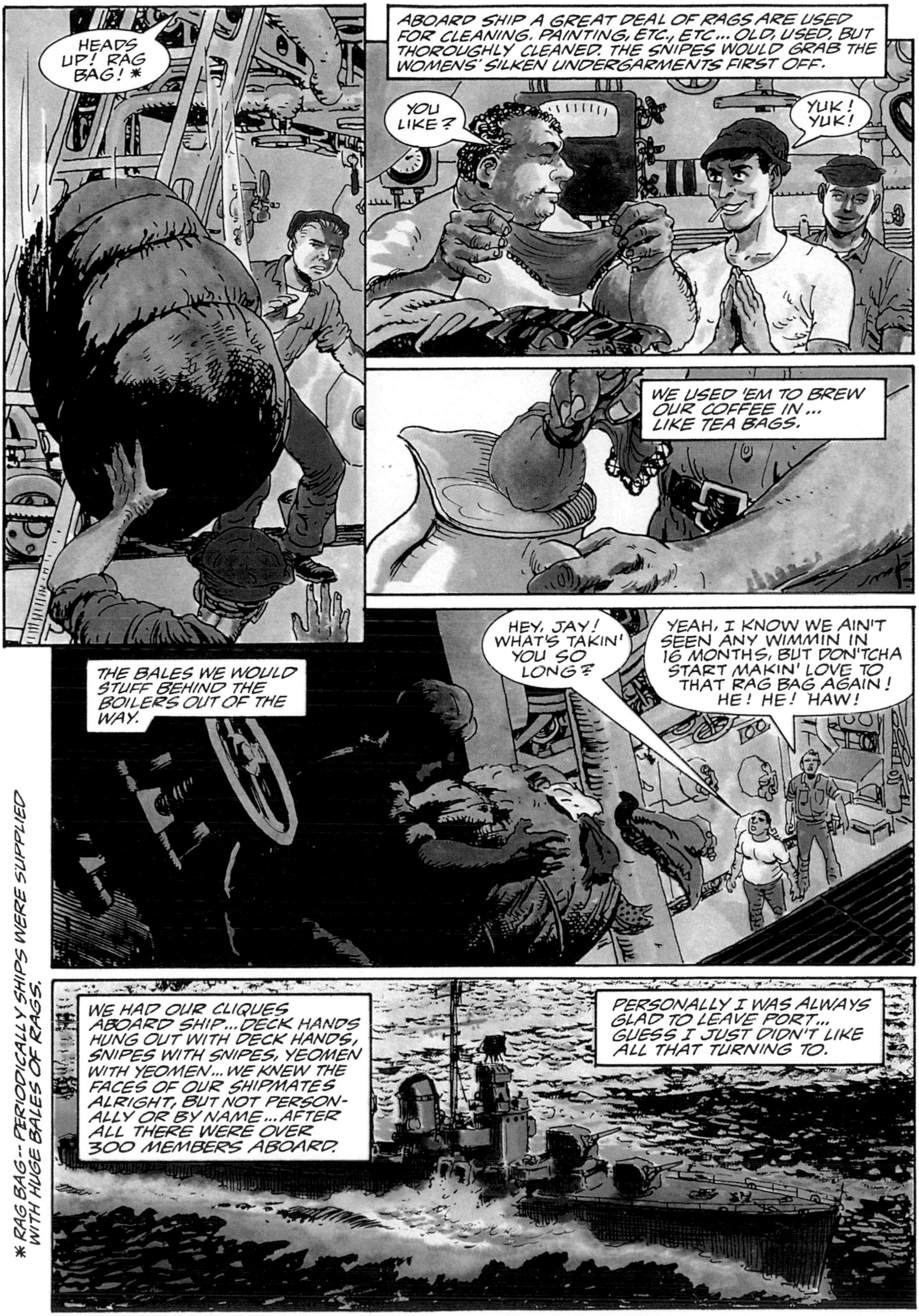
HEADS UP! RAG BAG! *
ABOARD SHIP A GREAT DEAL OF RAGS ARE USED FOR CLEANING, PAINTING, ETC., ETC... OLD, USED, BUT THOROUGHLY CLEANED. THE SNIPES WOULD GRAB THE WOMENS' SILKEN UNDERGARMENTS FIRST OFF.
YOU LIKE?
YUK! YUK!
WE USED 'EM TO BREW OUR COFFEE IN... LIKE TEA BAGS.
THE BALES WE WOULD STUFF BEHIND THE BOILERS OUT OF THE WAY.
HEY, JAY! WHAT'S TAKIN' YOU SO LONG?
YEAH, I KNOW WE AIN'T SEEN ANY WIMMIN IN 16 MONTHS, BUT DON'TCHA START MAKIN' LOVE TO THAT RAG BAG AGAIN! HE! HE! HAW!
WE HAD OUR CLIQUES ABOARD SHIP... DECK HANDS HUNG OUT WITH DECK HANDS, SNIPES WITH SNIPES, YEOMEN WITH YEOMEN... WE KNEW THE FACES OF OUR SHIPMATES ALRIGHT, BUT NOT PERSONALLY OR BY NAME... AFTER ALL THERE WERE OVER 300 MEMBERS ABOARD.
PERSONALLY I WAS ALWAYS GLAD TO LEAVE PORT... GUESS I JUST DIDN'T LIKE ALL THAT TURNING TO.

* RAG BAG-- PERIODICALLY SHIPS WERE SUPPLIED WITH HUGE BALES OF RAGS.

AT BRUNEI BAY WE ACTED AS AIR NAVIGATION SHIP FOR MINE-SWEEPERS AND PROVIDED FIRE SUPPORT... AFTER WHICH WE WERE BOUND FOR PARTS UNKNOWN... EVEN "SCUTTLEBUTT" COULDN'T FIGURE.

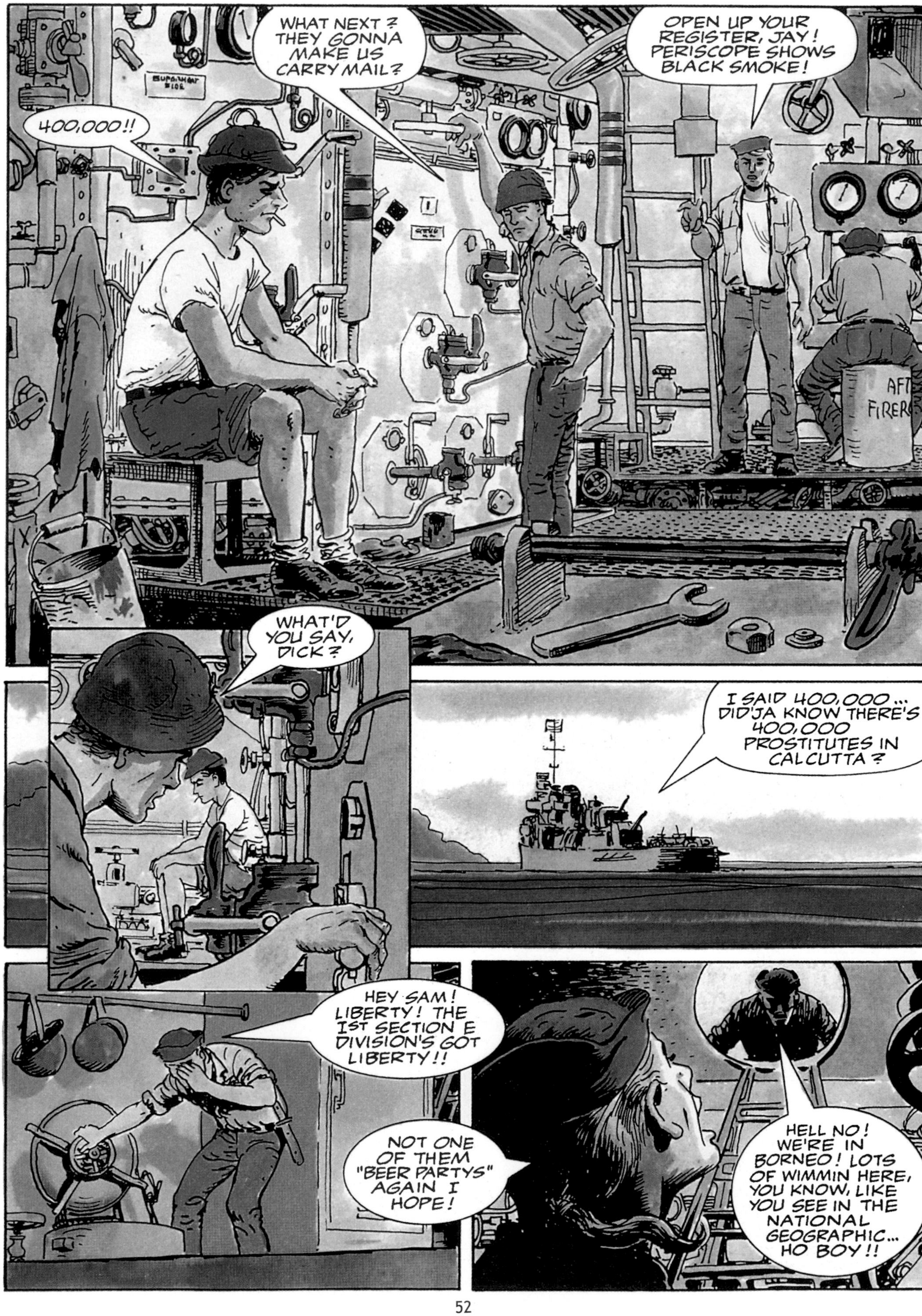
WHAT NEXT ? THEY GONNA MAKE US CARRY MAIL ?
OPEN UP YOUR REGISTER, JAY! PERISCOPE SHOWS BLACK SMOKE!
400,000!!
AFT FIRERO
WHAT'D YOU SAY, DICK ?
I SAID 400,000... DID'JA KNOW THERE'S 400,000 PROSTITUTES IN CALCUTTA ?
HEY SAM! LIBERTY! THE 1ST SECTION E DIVISION'S GOT LIBERTY!!
NOT ONE OF THEM "BEER PARTYS" AGAIN I HOPE!
HELL NO! WE'RE IN BORNEO! LOTS OF WIMMIN HERE, YOU KNOW, LIKE YOU SEE IN THE NATIONAL GEOGRAPHIC... HO BOY!!

FURTHER DOWN THE BEACH WE FOUND QUONSET HUTS...TENTS...TRUCKS...JEEPS... AND THE U.S. ARMY. THEY HAD A BASE THERE... AND A P.X. IT WOUND UP TO BE A GOOD LIBERTY...'CEPTIN' FOR THE LACK OF WOMEN.

...AND THEN, SEPTEMBER 2, 1945, THE NEWS CAME. JAPAN HAD SURRENDERED. WE WERE IN SUBIC BAY AT THE TIME. FRANKLY I DON'T REMEMBER ANY SHOUTING OR HOO-RAYS... THE ATOM BOMB? NEVER HEARD OF IT!

BY NOW I WAS A 2ND CLASS PO *, EQUIVALENT TO A STAFF SARGEANT IN THE ARMY AN' MAKING 96 BUCKS A MONTH. THE ENTIRE SHIP'S CREW GOT LIBERTY IN MANILA.

MANILA POST OFFICE

MANILA HAD BEEN HIT BAD. THE PEOPLE ...

RIZAL AVE.

...I DON'T KNOW WHERE THEY WERE...

SAN LUIS CHURCH

...WE SAW ONLY A COUPLE OF THEM ... SCURRYING AROUND THE RUBBLE.

I THINK I LIKE OUR "BEER" LIBERTIES BETTER!

* PO -- PETTY OFFICER.

SOMETIME IN SEPTEMBER WE LEFT THE AREA ...PROCEEDED TO BUCKNER BAY, OKINAWA, THEN TO THE YELLOW SEA.

HERE, ATTACHED TO THE 7TH FLEET, WE PROVIDED COVER FOR OCCUPATION LANDINGS IN THE NORTH CHINA-KOREA AREA. AROUND OCTOBER THE STEVENS WAS TIED UP TO A QUAY IN TSING-TAO, CHINA.

WITH ALL HOSTILITIES CEASED...THE SMOKING LAMP WAS ALWAYS LIT TOPSIDE....AN' WE EVEN HAD MOVIES ON DECK.

THE OFFICERS SAT IN FRONT ON CHAIRS. THE CREW BEHIND SAT ON WHATEVER THEY COULD.

ONE NIGHT DURING THE MOVIE, PINKY, ROSSO AND I WERE ON THE FANTAIL... SCHEMING.

WHEN THEY LET US OFF THE SHIP TOMORROW TO PLAY BALL, WE DUCK BEHIND THIS BRICK PILE...

...RUN ALONG THESE TRACKS BEHIND THIS WAREHOUSE...

...DOWN THE BREAK-WATER... PAST THE CHINESE BARRICADE...

WALLA!! TSING BABIES HERE WE COME!

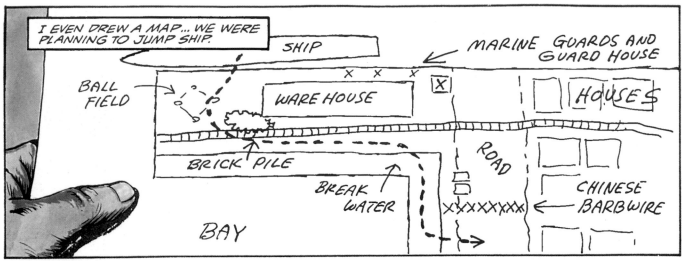

I EVEN DREW A MAP... WE WERE PLANNING TO JUMP SHIP.

SHIP

MARINE GUARDS AND GUARD HOUSE

BALL FIELD

WARE HOUSE

x x x

X

HOUSES

BRICK PILE

ROAD

BREAK WATER

CHINESE BARBWIRE

xxxxxxxx

BAY

LIBERTY WASN'T GRANTED IN TSINGTAO YET. THERE WERE STILL JAPANESE SOLDIERS IN THE TOWN WHO HADN'T BEEN EVACUATED AND THE NAVY FEARED AN "INCIDENT."

A CRUISER HAD SUPPLIED MARINE GUARDS STATIONED ON THE PIER TO PREVENT ANY UN-AUTHORIZED LIBERTY.

FURTHER UP THE QUAY A CHINESE BARRICADE WAS ALSO SET UP.

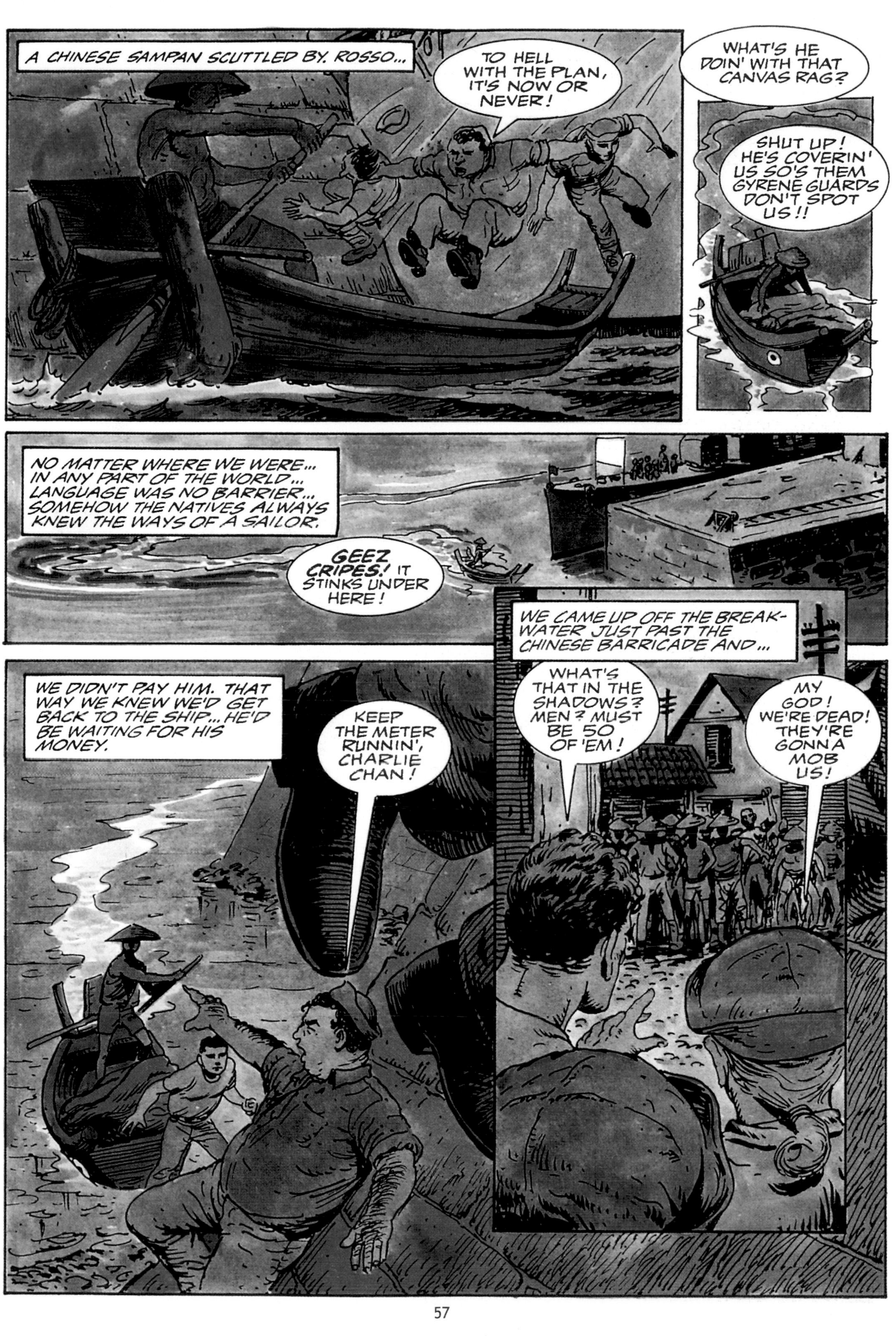
A CHINESE SAMPAN SCUTTLED BY. ROSSO...
TO HELL WITH THE PLAN, IT'S NOW OR NEVER!
WHAT'S HE DOIN' WITH THAT CANVAS RAG?
SHUT UP! HE'S COVERIN' US SO'S THEM GYRENE GUARDS DON'T SPOT US!!
NO MATTER WHERE WE WERE... IN ANY PART OF THE WORLD... LANGUAGE WAS NO BARRIER... SOMEHOW THE NATIVES ALWAYS KNEW THE WAYS OF A SAILOR.
GEEZ CRIPES! IT STINKS UNDER HERE!
WE DIDN'T PAY HIM. THAT WAY WE KNEW WE'D GET BACK TO THE SHIP... HE'D BE WAITING FOR HIS MONEY.
KEEP THE METER RUNNIN', CHARLIE CHAN!
WE CAME UP OFF THE BREAK-WATER JUST PAST THE CHINESE BARRICADE AND...
WHAT'S THAT IN THE SHADOWS? MEN? MUST BE 50 OF 'EM!
MY GOD! WE'RE DEAD! THEY'RE GONNA MOB US!

TURNED OUT THEY WERE RICKSHAW MEN...TAXI DRIVERS... EACH WANTED US AS A FARE... AN' THEY NEARLY TORE US APART FIGHTING OVER US.

ROSSO'S CAB WENT THAT WAY... PINKY'S THIS WAY... AN' MINE BARRELED UP A HILL... BOY, COULD THOSE GUYS RUN! ... FOREVER!!

TO MAKE A LONG STORY SHORT, MY CAB DROPPED ME OFF AT THE NEW YORK BAR... YEAH!! IN CHINA!! THAT'S WHAT THE SIGN SAID! ROSSO'S AND PINKY'S CABS WERE ALREADY THERE ...

...IN FACT THEY WERE ALREADY UPSTAIRS IN BED, UNDER SILK SHEETS! FOR 53 CENTS WE SPENT ONE BEAUTIFUL NIGHT IN TSINGTAO.

RETURNING NEXT MORNING WE FOUND TWO OTHER CANS HAD TIED UP ALONGSIDE OURS DUR-ING THE NIGHT. BEFORE NOON ALL THREE CANS HEARD ABOUT THE NEW YORK BAR.

THAT FOLLOWING NIGHT...FOUR MEN FROM ONE OF THE OTHER CANS PULLED THE SAME STUNT... AND DIDN'T RETURN.

THEY GOT TO THE NEW YORK BAR ALRIGHT... BUT DECIDED TO DO SOME SIGHT SEEING.

BUT A CRAZED, DELIRIOUS FIGURE STILL FIGHTING AN INSANE WAR STEPPED IN FRONT OF THEM...IT HAPPENED... AFTER THE WAR... IN TSINGTAO, CHINA.

ON NOVEMBER 7, 1945 THE STEVENS RETURNED TO THE UNITED STATES AND SAN DIEGO.

59

THE WAR HAD BEEN OVER ALMOST THREE MONTHS, AND SO...WE MISSED OUT ON THE PARADES...

...THE FREE BEERS AN' FUN LOVIN' WOMEN. THERE WAS NO ONE TO GREET US.

WITH MUSTER OUT PAPERS IN HAND, AFTER 3 YEARS OF OVERSEAS DUTY I SALUTED MY FLAG AND SHIP FOR THE LAST TIME.

IT WAS A LONG-TRAIN RIDE TO NEW YORK. CLEAR ACROSS THE STATES...

...MY THOUGHTS WERE OF BEAUTY WAITING...HOW HAPPY SHE WOULD BE TO SEE ME.

REPORTING TO LIDO BEACH, LONG ISLAND I WAS FORMALLY DISCHARGED AND RETURNED TO MY MOUNTAIN HOME. A FRESH GRAVE WAS AT THE GARDEN GATE.

BEAUTY
A GOOD DOG

SHE WAS A YOUNG DOG, PETE. WHAT HAPPENED? ...HOW'D SHE GET KILLED?

SHE WASN'T KILLED, SAM. I GUESS SHE JUST... DIED.

FINIS

SAM GLANZMAN

60

A Sailor's Story
Book II

Winds, Dreams, and Dragons

OTHERS, ON HITTING, FAILING TO EXPLODE, PILED UP LIKE SO MUCH TRASH...

...TAKING ON MANY GROTESQUE SHAPES.

A PHOENIX SQUATTED IN A NEST OF ITS OWN FIRE-BLACKENED WRECKAGE.

AMPUTATED TAILS AND WINGS...

...RUPTURED GAS TANKS...

...CRIMSON SHEETS OF FIRE RAGING THROUGH SUPERSTRUCTURES...

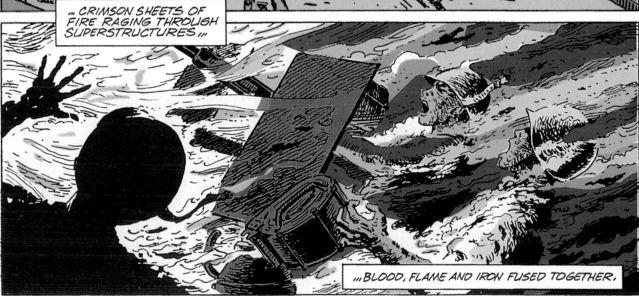

...BLOOD, FLAME AND IRON FUSED TOGETHER.

BROKEN SHIPS ... BLEEDING INTERNALLY ... STAGGERING, HALF-DEAD ...

... PLANES SHOT TO PIECES ... COUGHING SMOKE ... FALLING APART ...

... DYING SEAMEN ... TORN AND SHREDDED BODIES ... SPLINTERED BONES ...

DECAPITATED KIKUSUI PILOTS CATAPULTING FROM CRASHING AIRCRAFT ... CARNAGE.

That was the kamikaze, "the divine wind," unimagined earlier in the war. Near war's end, it burst forth, as unexpected as an exploding bomb . . .detonating in all its fury over Okinawa in 1945. But, in the early stages of the war, Japanese employed conventional tactics against ships and Japanese dive bombing was the most accurate in the world.

SO IT WAS THAT IN 1943, THE KAMIKAZE, THE DIVINE WIND WAS UNKNOWN. IN AUGUST 1943, A DIFFERENT WIND BLEW ACROSS THE BOW OF THE U.S.S. STEVENS.

...A GENTLE PACIFIC WIND THAT SOFTLY CARESSED HER AS SHE SLID ALMOST SILENTLY THROUGH THE BLACK WATERS. IT WAS NIGHT, PITCH DARK, AND ALTHOUGH WE COULD NOT SEE, WE KNEW WE WERE PASSING AN ISLAND. WE ALWAYS KNEW, IF THIS GENTLE WIND WAS BLOWING.

SWEEPING OVER AN ISLAND, THE WIND CARRIED WITH IT THE ISLAND'S FRAGRANCE...GARDENIAS AND OTHER TROPICAL FLOWERS... A HEAVY, SWEET AROMA THAT WOULD HOVER OVER OUR SHIP LIKE A MANTLE.

THE MEN TOPSIDE WOULD BECOME VERY QUIET. THIS WIND SEEMED TO HAVE A NARCOTIC EFFECT, LULLING THEM INTO A HYPNOTIC DREAM WORLD... A WORLD OF PEACE AND HOME.

BILLY B. WILSON, A LONER... MOODY... MELANCHOLY... HAD HIS DREAMS.

HE WAS FROM KANSAS, A COWBOY. HIS DREAMS WERE OF FLASH, HIS HORSE, AND RALPH, AN INDIAN FRIEND.

HE WAS ON OUR SHIP FOR ABOUT A YEAR I GUESS... AN' THEN HE WAS TRANSFERRED. ONE NIGHT SOMETHING HAPPENED TO HIM... HIS RIGHT SIDE BECAME PARALYZED AN' HIS FACE FROZE INTO A PERMANENT TWISTED MASK... BILLY B. MUST 'A' SLIPPED INTO HIS DREAMS.

68

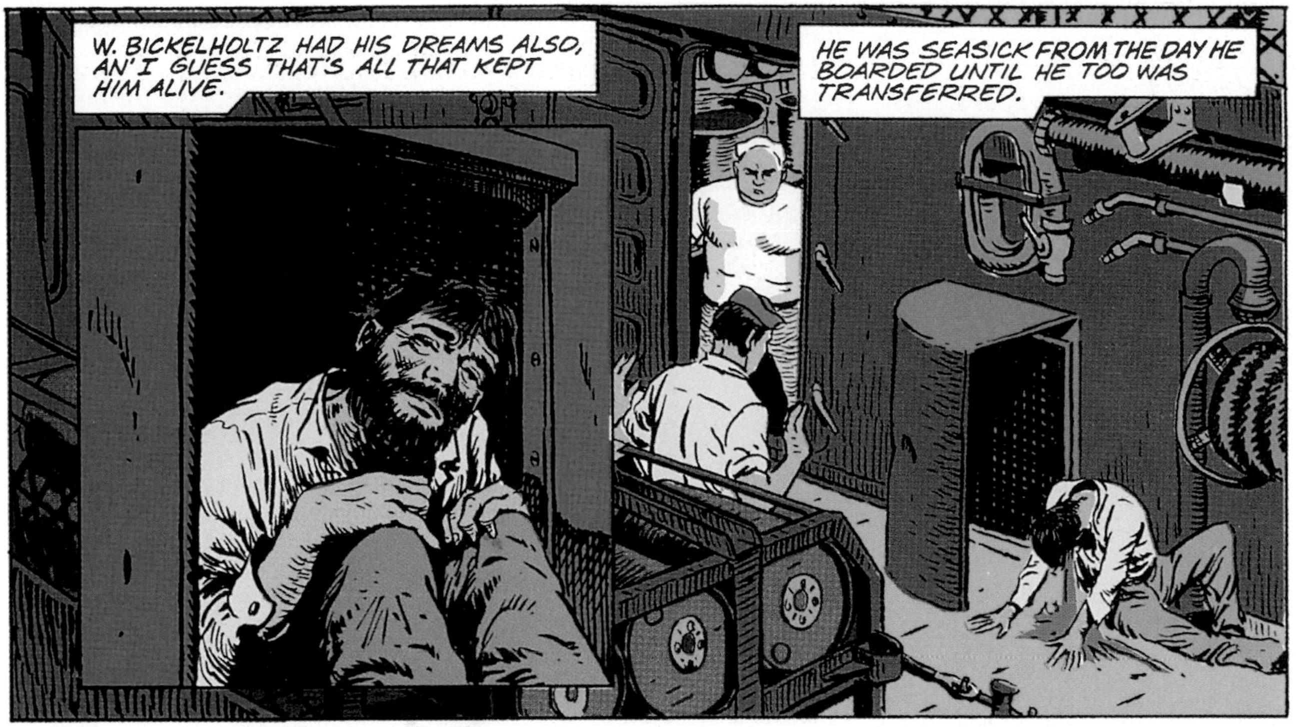
W. BICKELHOLTZ HAD HIS DREAMS ALSO, AN' I GUESS THAT'S ALL THAT KEPT HIM ALIVE.
HE WAS SEASICK FROM THE DAY HE BOARDED UNTIL HE TOO WAS TRANSFERRED.

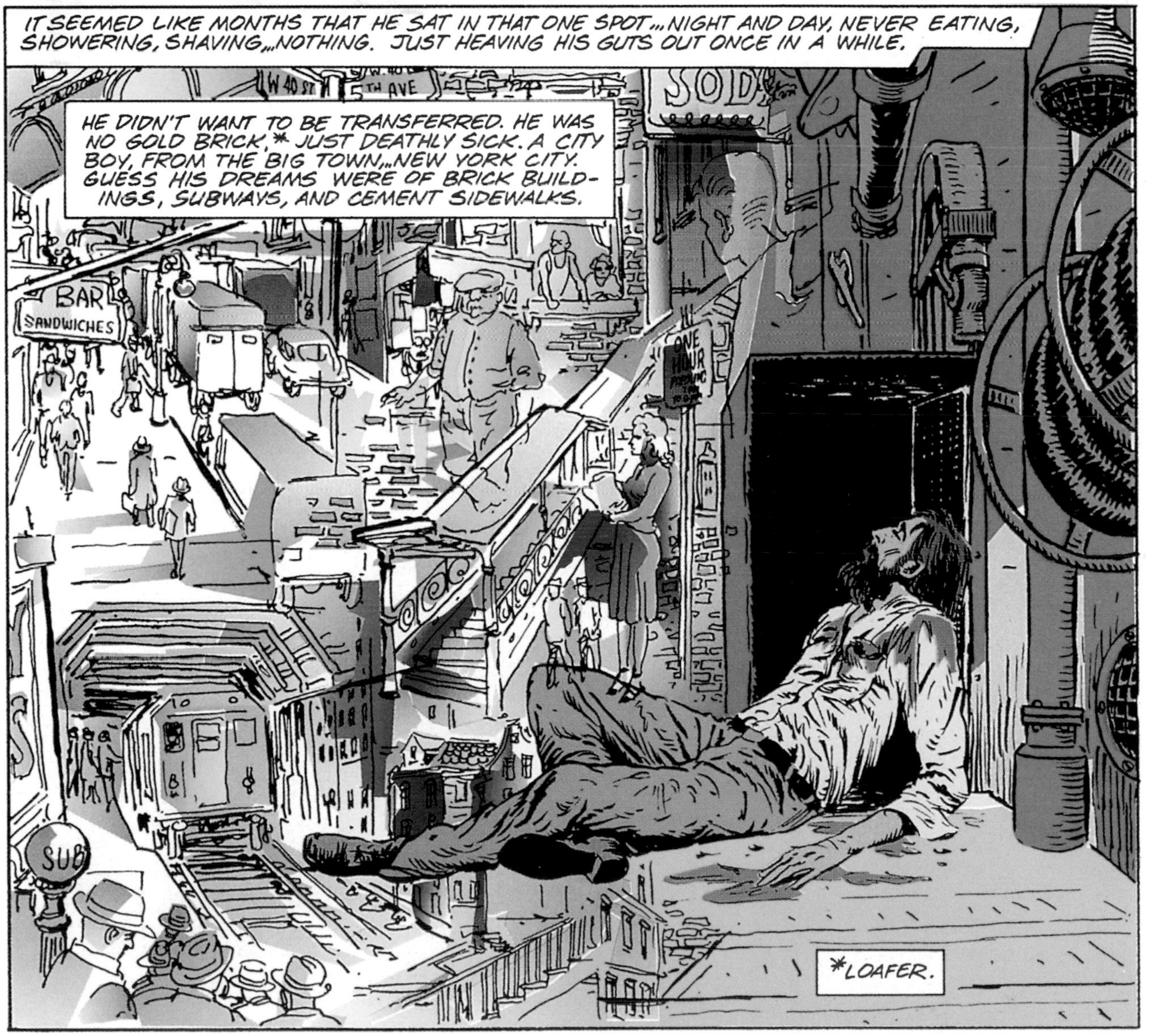
IT SEEMED LIKE MONTHS THAT HE SAT IN THAT ONE SPOT... NIGHT AND DAY, NEVER EATING, SHOWERING, SHAVING... NOTHING. JUST HEAVING HIS GUTS OUT ONCE IN A WHILE.
HE DIDN'T WANT TO BE TRANSFERRED. HE WAS NO GOLD BRICK,* JUST DEATHLY SICK. A CITY BOY, FROM THE BIG TOWN... NEW YORK CITY. GUESS HIS DREAMS WERE OF BRICK BUILDINGS, SUBWAYS, AND CEMENT SIDEWALKS.
W 40 ST
5TH AVE
BAR
SANDWICHES
ONE HOUR
SUB
*LOAFER.

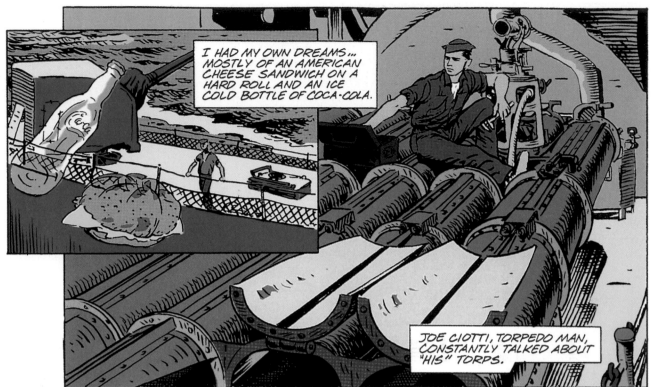

I HAD MY OWN DREAMS... MOSTLY OF AN AMERICAN CHEESE SANDWICH ON A HARD ROLL AND AN ICE COLD BOTTLE OF COCA-COLA.

JOE CIOTTI, TORPEDO MAN, CONSTANTLY TALKED ABOUT "HIS" TORPS.

I KNOW HIS DREAMS WERE OF KNOCKING OUT A JAPANESE CRUISER.

BUCK? BUCK TALBERT? WHO KNOWS WHAT HIS DREAMS WERE... BUCK HIMSELF PROBABLY DIDN'T KNOW. HE WAS WHAT WE CALLED "ASIATIC"--TOO MUCH TIME IN THE ASIAN THEATER OF OPERATIONS.

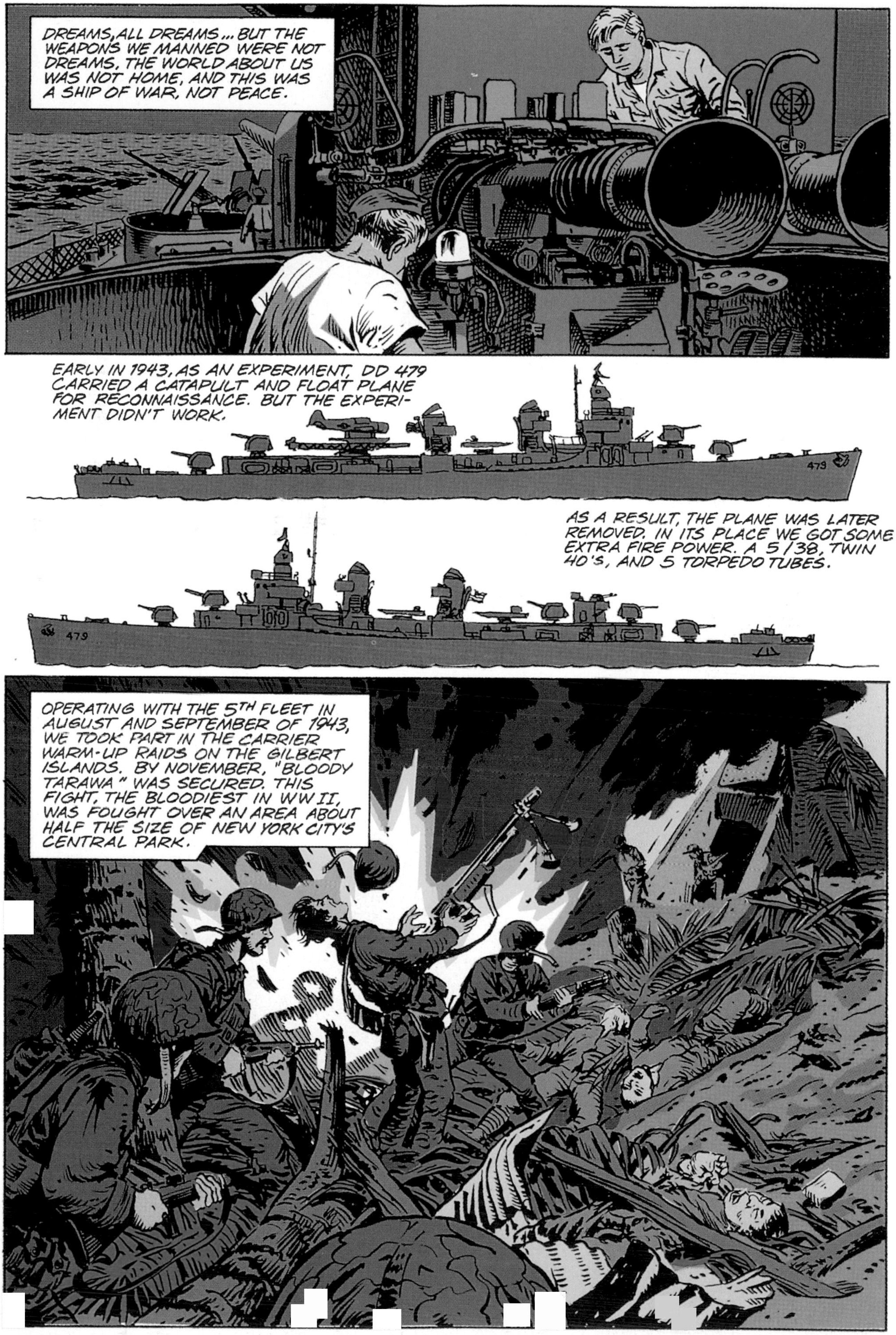
DREAMS, ALL DREAMS ... BUT THE WEAPONS WE MANNED WERE NOT DREAMS. THE WORLD ABOUT US WAS NOT HOME, AND THIS WAS A SHIP OF WAR, NOT PEACE.
EARLY IN 1943, AS AN EXPERIMENT, DD 479 CARRIED A CATAPULT AND FLOAT PLANE FOR RECONNAISSANCE. BUT THE EXPERIMENT DIDN'T WORK.
479
AS A RESULT, THE PLANE WAS LATER REMOVED. IN ITS PLACE WE GOT SOME EXTRA FIRE POWER. A 5/38, TWIN 40'S, AND 5 TORPEDO TUBES.
479
OPERATING WITH THE 5TH FLEET IN AUGUST AND SEPTEMBER OF 1943, WE TOOK PART IN THE CARRIER WARM-UP RAIDS ON THE GILBERT ISLANDS. BY NOVEMBER, "BLOODY TARAWA" WAS SECURED. THIS FIGHT, THE BLOODIEST IN WW II, WAS FOUGHT OVER AN AREA ABOUT HALF THE SIZE OF NEW YORK CITY'S CENTRAL PARK.

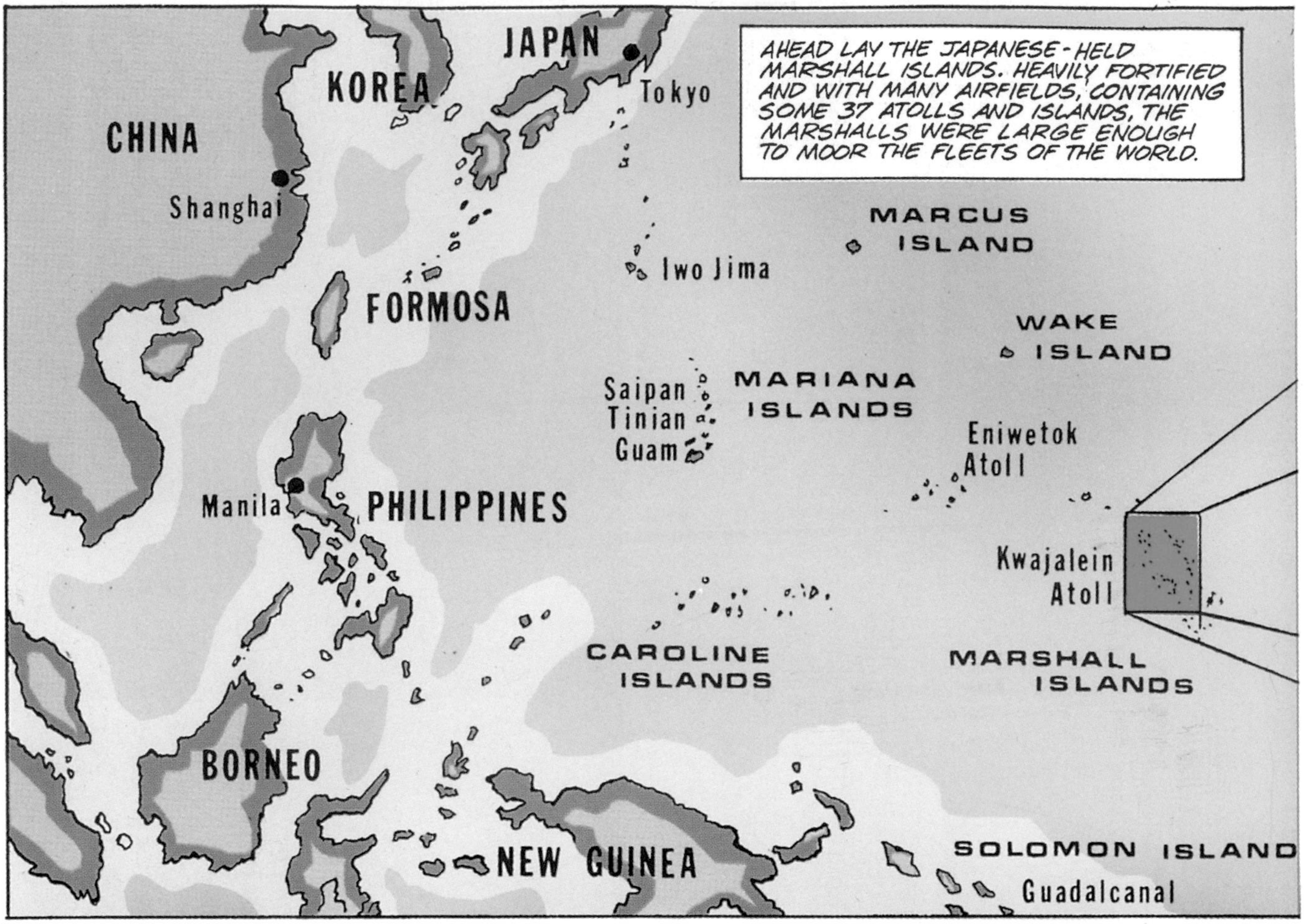
AHEAD LAY THE JAPANESE-HELD MARSHALL ISLANDS. HEAVILY FORTIFIED AND WITH MANY AIRFIELDS, CONTAINING SOME 37 ATOLLS AND ISLANDS, THE MARSHALLS WERE LARGE ENOUGH TO MOOR THE FLEETS OF THE WORLD.
JAPAN
KOREA
Tokyo
CHINA
Shanghai
MARCUS ISLAND
Iwo Jima
FORMOSA
WAKE ISLAND
Saipan
Tinian
Guam
MARIANA ISLANDS
Eniwetok Atoll
Manila
PHILIPPINES
Kwajalein Atoll
CAROLINE ISLANDS
MARSHALL ISLANDS
BORNEO
NEW GUINEA
SOLOMON ISLAND
Guadalcanal

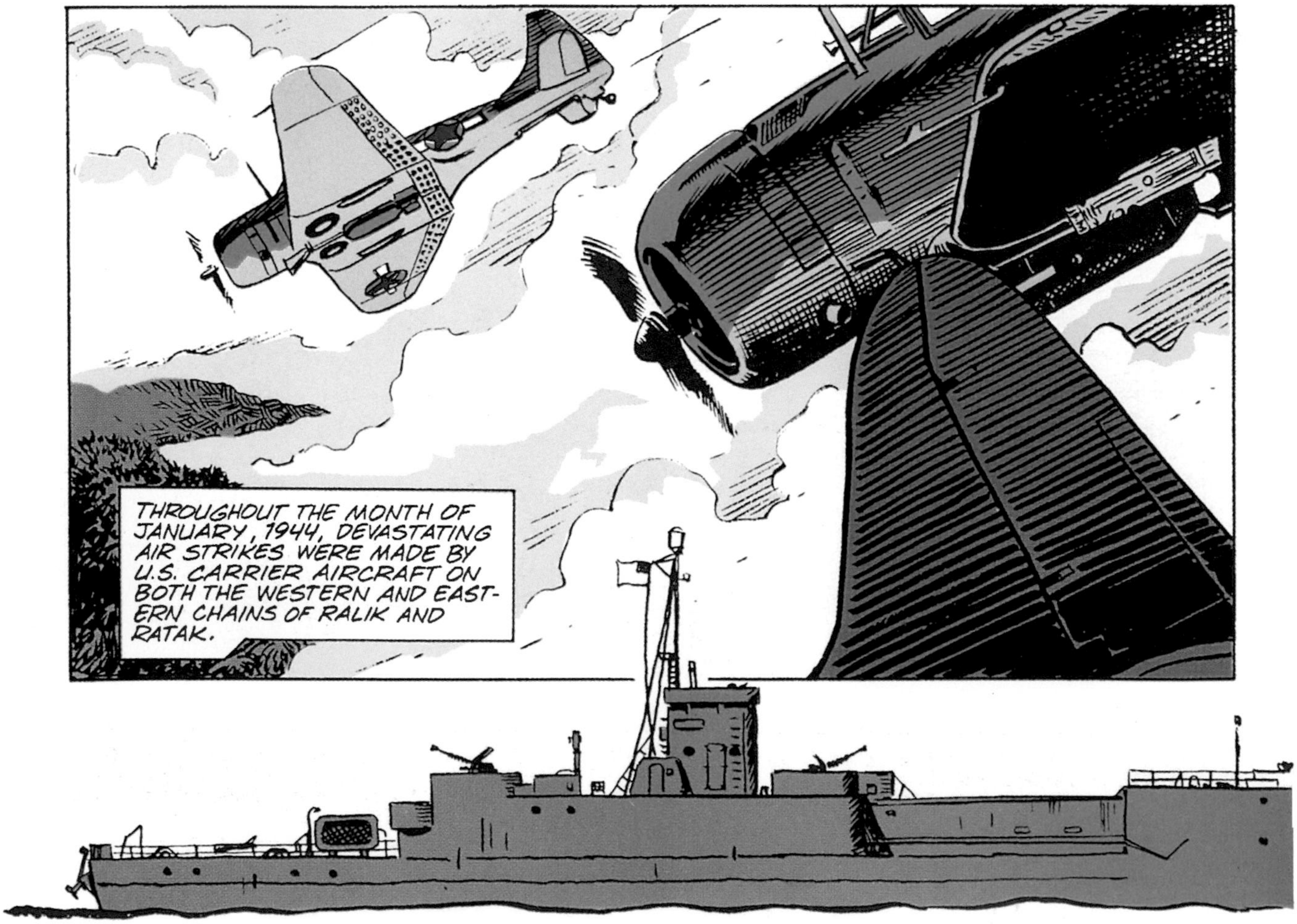
THROUGHOUT THE MONTH OF JANUARY, 1944, DEVASTATING AIR STRIKES WERE MADE BY U.S. CARRIER AIRCRAFT ON BOTH THE WESTERN AND EASTERN CHAINS OF RALIK AND RATAK.

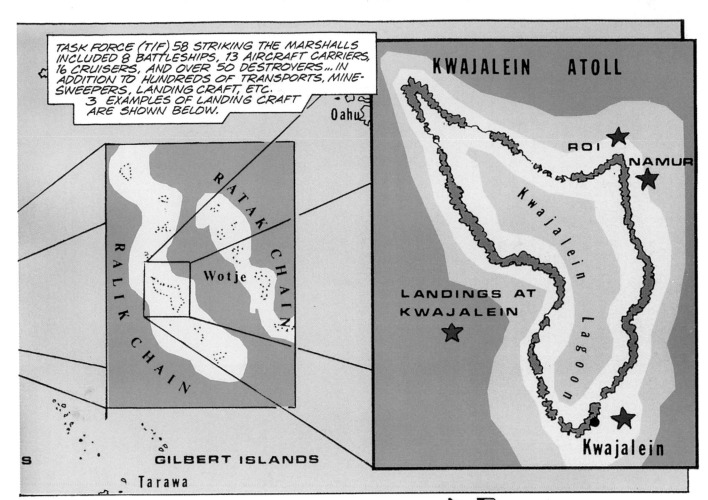

TASK FORCE (T/F) 58 STRIKING THE MARSHALLS
INCLUDED 8 BATTLESHIPS, 13 AIRCRAFT CARRIERS,
16 CRUISERS, AND OVER 50 DESTROYERS... IN
ADDITION TO HUNDREDS OF TRANSPORTS, MINE-
SWEEPERS, LANDING CRAFT, ETC.
     3 EXAMPLES OF LANDING CRAFT
     ARE SHOWN BELOW.

KWAJALEIN ATOLL

ROI

NAMUR

Kwajalein Lagoon

LANDINGS AT
KWAJALEIN

Kwajalein

Oahu

RATAK CHAIN

RALIK CHAIN

Wotje

GILBERT ISLANDS

Tarawa

THE LVT (LANDING VEHICLE,
TRACKED) SHOWN IS THE
ASSAULT VERSION THAT
HAD AN M3 TANK TURRET
TO PROVIDE FIRE SUPPORT
IN THE FIRST STAGE OF
LANDING. THE LVT 4 VER-
SION HAD A LOADING RAMP
IN THE REAR FOR JEEPS
OR LIGHT ARTILLERY.

THE DUKW* SHOWN WAS
USED AS A LOGISTICAL
STORES CARRIER. IT
FERRIED SUPPLIES FROM
SHIPS OFFSHORE TO
SUPPLY DUMPS INLAND.

*MANUFACTURER'S CODE

D – 1942
U – UTILITY
K – TWIN REAR WHEELS
W – ALL-WHEEL DRIVE

408

THE LCI (LANDING-CRAFT INFANTRY) SHOWN WAS AN OCEAN-GOING ASSAULT VESSEL
WHICH HAD A RANGE OF 4,000 MILES AT 12 KNOTS. IT CARRIED UPWARDS TO 200
TROOPS. LARGELY UNSUNG (OFTEN CALLED "PALL BEARERS"), AMPHIBIOUS VESSELS
SUCH AS THIS AND THEIR CREWS MADE THE INVASIONS POSSIBLE.

ON JANUARY 30TH, ATTACHED TO TASK GROUP (TG) 52.8, THE U.S.S. STEVENS JOINED IN THE ASSAULT AS EVERYTHING FROM 16-INCH SHELLS FROM BATTLESHIPS TO THE "KITCHEN SINK" WAS HURLED AT KWAJALEIN.

SIMULTANEOUSLY, SURFACE SHIPS MADE A DIVERSIONARY ATTACK ON THE EASTERN CHAIN ... ESPECIALLY WELL-FORTIFIED WOTJE. SO BADLY MAULED WERE THESE JAPANESE FORCES, THAT AFTERWARD, THEY COULD GIVE NO ASSISTANCE TO KWAJALEIN, WHERE THE REAL ASSAULT STRUCK.

16 INCH BREECH BLOCK AND PLUG

LITERALLY BLOWN OUT OF THE JAPANESE EMPIRE, KWAJALEIN WAS STRIPPED CLEAN. NOT A PALM TREE WAS LEFT STANDING. A TORNADO OF EXPLO- SIVES FELL.

SHORE BATTERIES WERE RIPPED FROM EMPLACE-MENTS, BOMB-PROOF SHELTERS AND CONCRETE BARRIERS WERE SMASHED TO RUBBLE. EXPOSED IN FOXHOLES AND TRENCHES, JAPANESE SOLDIERS HAD THEIR NECKS BROKEN BY THE BLASTS.

600 YARDS OFF SHORE, 24 LCI'S EQUIPPED WITH ROCKETS DELUGED THE LANDING BEACHES. DESTROY-ERS MOVED IN TO THEIR LINES OF DEPARTURE. LTV'S AND DUKW'S CROSSED THE REEFS AS AMERICAN TROOPS POURED ONTO THE ISLAND WITH TANKS AND EQUIPMENT.

SHOWN BELOW IS A TYPICAL FIRE SUPPORT FOR AMPHIBIOUS LANDINGS:

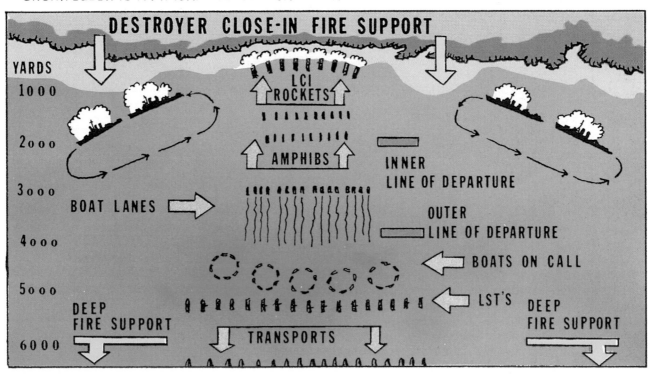

DESTROYER CLOSE-IN FIRE SUPPORT

YARDS

1000 — LCI ROCKETS

2000 — AMPHIBS — INNER LINE OF DEPARTURE

3000 — BOAT LANES — OUTER LINE OF DEPARTURE

4000 — BOATS ON CALL

5000 — LST'S

DEEP FIRE SUPPORT — TRANSPORTS — DEEP FIRE SUPPORT

6000

CLOSE INSHORE, AN LCI WAS GETTING THE STUFFIN'S POUNDED OUT OF IT.

TEARING IN AT FLANK SPEED TO GIVE ASSISTANCE, OUR SHIP BANGED AWAY AT SHORE BATTERIES.

SOME OF THE STEVENS CREW NOT AT GUN STATIONS SAUNTERED OVER TO THE STARBOARD SIDE TO SEE THE "SHOW"...MUCH TO THE DISMAY OF OUR SKIPPER...

...WHO PROMPTLY INFORMED THE "SIGHTSEERS"...

ALL HANDS!! ANYONE DESIRING A PURPLE HEART, LAY UP TO THE STARBOARD SIDE!

ALTHOUGH WE HAD SILENCED THE SHORE BATTERIES, WE WERE SO CLOSE INSHORE THAT THE JAPANESE WERE SCORING HITS ON OUR STARBOARD SIDE WITH RIFLE FIRE, THE CREW HAD BEEN UNAWARE OF THIS UNTIL THE CAPTAIN'S "ANNOUNCEMENT."

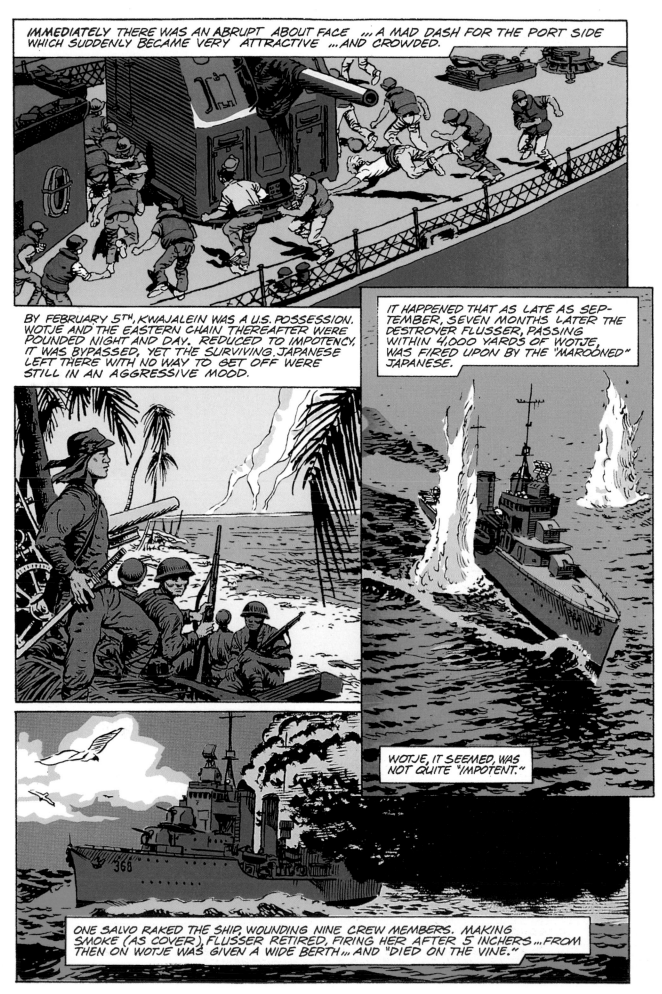

IMMEDIATELY THERE WAS AN ABRUPT ABOUT FACE ... A MAD DASH FOR THE PORT SIDE WHICH SUDDENLY BECAME VERY ATTRACTIVE ... AND CROWDED.

BY FEBRUARY 5TH, KWAJALEIN WAS A U.S. POSSESSION. WOTJE AND THE EASTERN CHAIN THEREAFTER WERE POUNDED NIGHT AND DAY. REDUCED TO IMPOTENCY, IT WAS BYPASSED, YET THE SURVIVING JAPANESE LEFT THERE WITH NO WAY TO GET OFF WERE STILL IN AN AGGRESSIVE MOOD.

IT HAPPENED THAT AS LATE AS SEPTEMBER, SEVEN MONTHS LATER THE DESTROYER FLUSSER, PASSING WITHIN 4,000 YARDS OF WOTJE, WAS FIRED UPON BY THE "MAROONED" JAPANESE.

WOTJE, IT SEEMED, WAS NOT QUITE "IMPOTENT."

ONE SALVO RAKED THE SHIP, WOUNDING NINE CREW MEMBERS. MAKING SMOKE (AS COVER), FLUSSER RETIRED, FIRING HER AFTER 5 INCHERS ... FROM THEN ON WOTJE WAS GIVEN A WIDE BERTH ... AND "DIED ON THE VINE."

DD 479

U.S.S. STEVENS (TRAVEL LOG)

FEBRUARY
4 UNDERWAY FROM MARSHALLS
8 ARRIVED FUNA FUTI, ELLICE ISLANDS.
13 DEPARTED FUNA FUTI.
15 ARRIVED GUADALCANAL.
16,17,18. PATROL DUTY.
19 DEPARTED GUADALCANAL.
22 ARRIVED NOUMEA, NEW CALEDONIA.
28 DEPARTED NOUMEA.

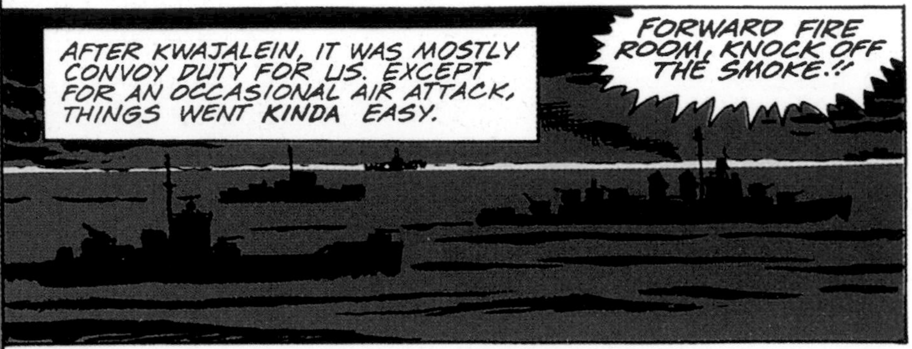
AFTER KWAJALEIN, IT WAS MOSTLY CONVOY DUTY FOR US. EXCEPT FOR AN OCCASIONAL AIR ATTACK, THINGS WENT KINDA EASY.
FORWARD FIRE ROOM, KNOCK OFF THE SMOKE.!!

EXCEPT WHEN USED AS A SMOKE SCREEN, A U.S. SHIP OF WAR NEVER MAKES SMOKE. FIRST, IT IS UNECONOMICAL... AN INDICATION OF TOO MUCH OIL BEING BURNED. SECOND, IT IS DETRIMENTAL TO FIRE BOXES AND WATER TUBES. THIRD, THE SHIP WOULD BE COVERED WITH BLACK OILY SOOT, AND FOURTH, AN ENEMY SHIP COULD SPOT THE POSITION OF A SHIP STEAMING EVEN WELL BELOW THE HORIZON.

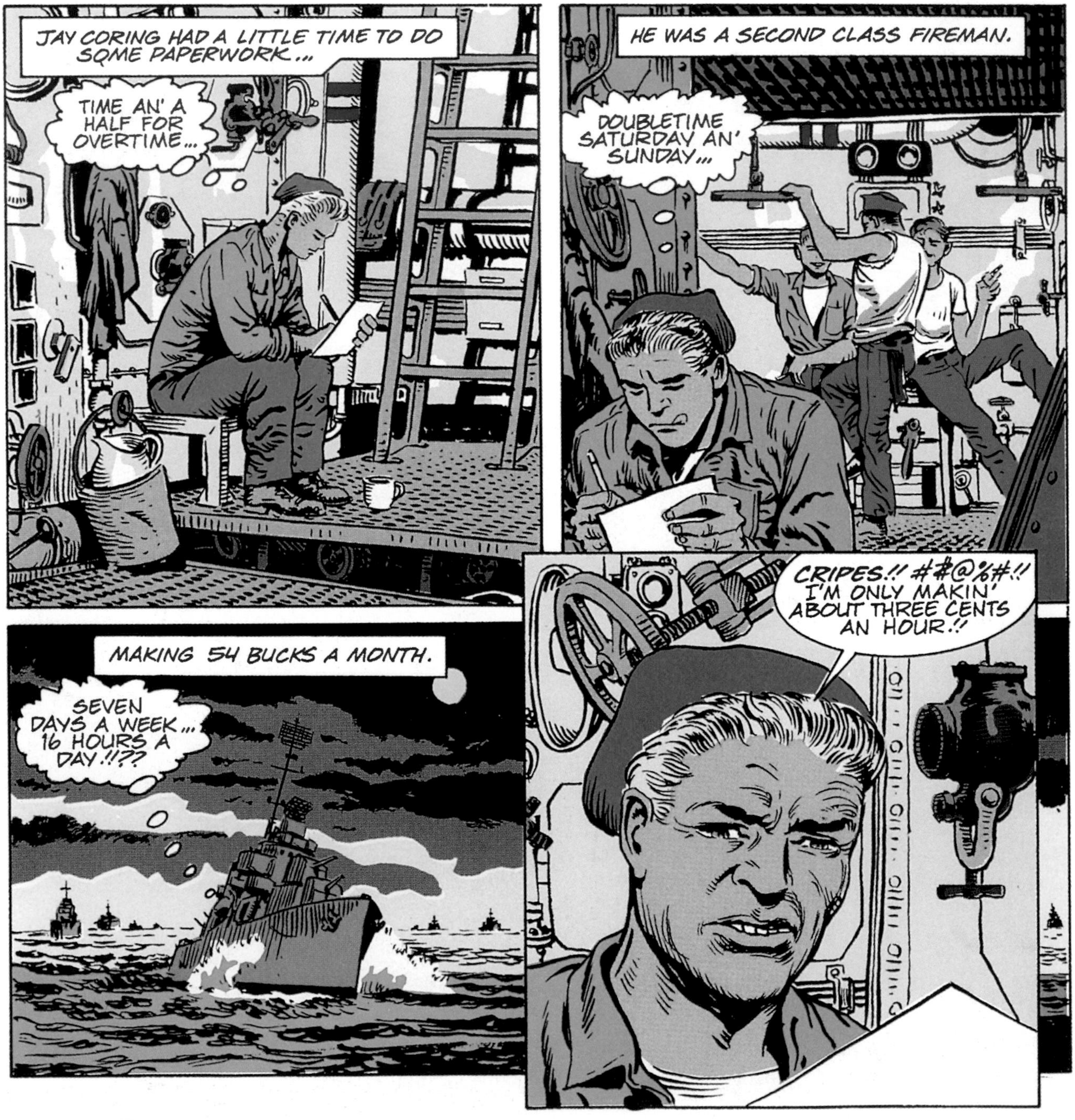
JAY CORING HAD A LITTLE TIME TO DO SOME PAPERWORK...
TIME AN' A HALF FOR OVERTIME...
HE WAS A SECOND CLASS FIREMAN.
DOUBLETIME SATURDAY AN' SUNDAY...
MAKING 54 BUCKS A MONTH.
SEVEN DAYS A WEEK... 16 HOURS A DAY!!??
CRIPES!! #$@%#!! I'M ONLY MAKIN' ABOUT THREE CENTS AN HOUR.!!

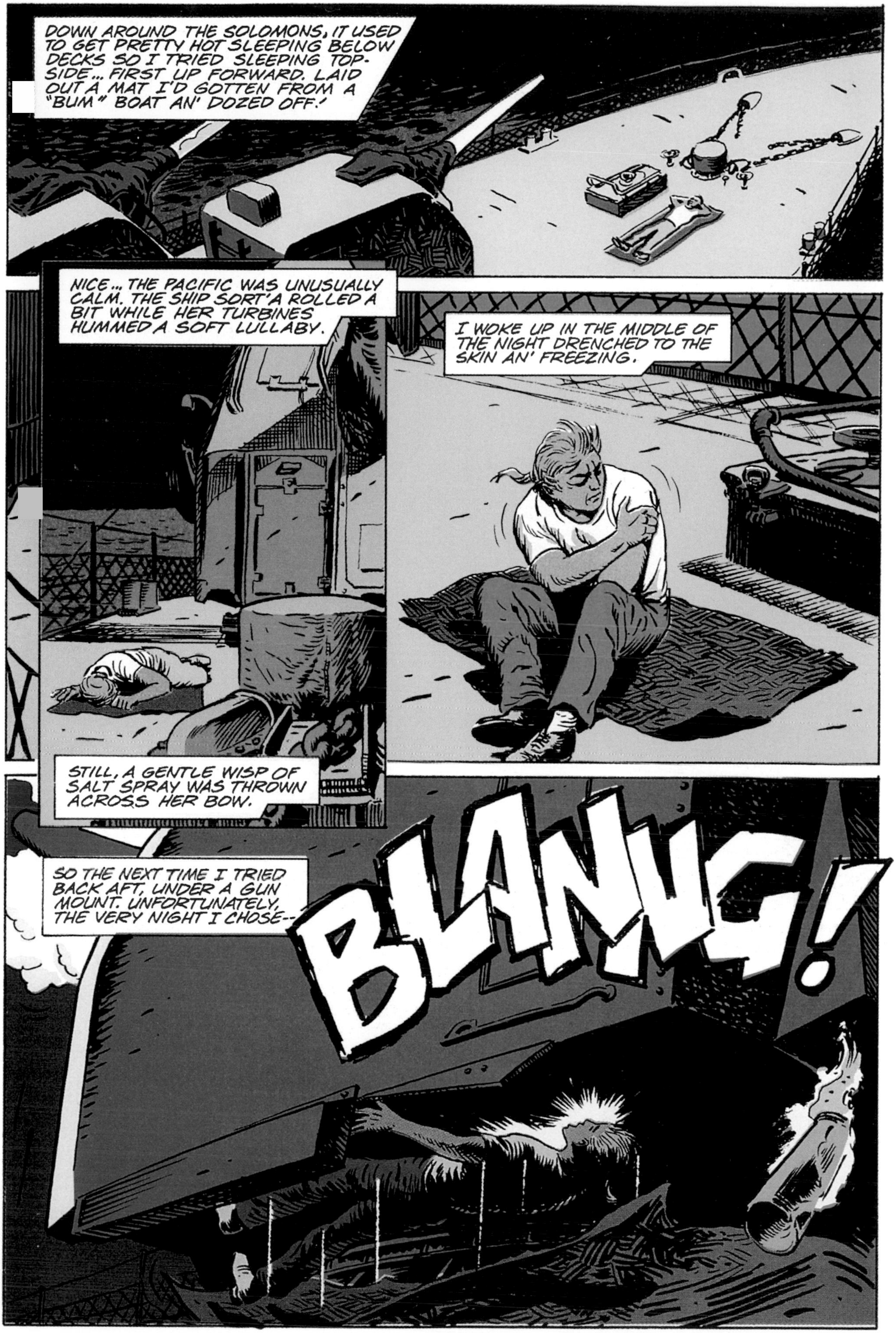

DOWN AROUND THE SOLOMONS, IT USED TO GET PRETTY HOT SLEEPING BELOW DECKS SO I TRIED SLEEPING TOP-SIDE... FIRST UP FORWARD. LAID OUT A MAT I'D GOTTEN FROM A "BUM" BOAT AN' DOZED OFF!
NICE... THE PACIFIC WAS UNUSUALLY CALM. THE SHIP SORT'A ROLLED A BIT WHILE HER TURBINES HUMMED A SOFT LULLABY.
STILL, A GENTLE WISP OF SALT SPRAY WAS THROWN ACROSS HER BOW.
I WOKE UP IN THE MIDDLE OF THE NIGHT DRENCHED TO THE SKIN AN' FREEZING.
SO THE NEXT TIME I TRIED BACK AFT, UNDER A GUN MOUNT. UNFORTUNATELY, THE VERY NIGHT I CHOSE--
BLANUG!

WE HAD BEEN IN CONVOY SCREENING WITH TWO OTHER CANS WHEN OUR SHIP'S RADAR PICKED UP AN ENEMY PLANE AND FIRED ON IT.

I WAS QUITE DEAF FOR SOME TIME AFTER, BUT I'LL NEVER FORGET THAT SIGHT! **BLANNG!!** BEAUTIFUL! ONE SHELL AN' THAT PLANE JUST DISAPPEARED IN A BALL OF FIRE!

I GUESS GENERAL QUARTERS SOUNDED AT THE SAME TIME. I DON'T KNOW. LIKE I SAID, I WAS DEAF.

BUT ALL HANDS WERE WIDE AWAKE RUNNING TO QUARTERS ... NOT FULLY CLOTHED, BUT WIDE AWAKE.

SUDDENLY, ONE OF THE OTHER CANS ACCIDENTALLY (?) FIRED A STAR SHELL.

FOR SEVERAL MINUTES THE ENTIRE WORLD WAS LIT UP. IT WAS THE SCARIEST MOMENT OF MY LIFE. WE WERE EXPOSED LIKE COCKROACHES ON A WHITE SHEET.

NOW WE DEFINITELY DIDN'T NEED THAT. THE DARKNESS GAVE ALL THE SHIPS GOOD COVER AN' WE WERE FIRING WITH RADAR.

HOLY HANNAH! WHAT THE @#!✕%! THEY DOIN'?

THE PLANE WE CLOBBERED MUST'VE BEEN ON A LONE RECONNAISSANCE, OR MAYBE LOST. ANYWAY, NO OTHERS SHOWED UP AND, IN TIME, WE SECURED FROM G.Q.

I WENT BELOW... HIT MY SACK, AN' SWORE NEVER, EVER TO SLEEP UNDER A GUN MOUNT AGAIN.

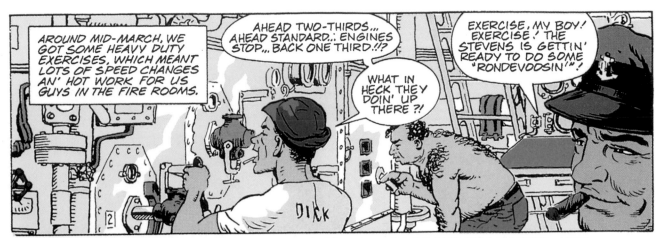

INDEED WE WERE. WE RENDEZVOUSED WITH T/F37 TO BOMBARD THE KAVIENG AREA OF NORTHWESTERN NEW IRELAND.

THE TENNESSEE AS SHE APPEARED IN 1944:

WE HAD SOME FINE COMPANY THAT DAY: FOUR ESCORT CARRIERS, FOURTEEN DESTROYERS, AND FOUR BATTLESHIPS (CALLED "WAGONS").

THESE "WAGONS" WERE THE BATTLE-SHIPS IDAHO (BB42) AND MISSISSIPPI (BB41). BOTH WERE ON THE EAST COAST, AS WAS BATTLESHIP NEW MEXICO (BB40), WHEN WAR BROKE OUT. IMMEDIATELY, THESE THREE HAD BEEN SENT TO THE PACIFIC TO BEEF UP OUR WEST COAST DEFENSE.

TENNESSEE REJOINED THE FLEET QUICKLY BECAUSE OF HER LIGHT DAMAGE. SHE IS SHOWN HERE AS SHE APPEARED EARLY IN 1942.

AT PEARL HARBOR, DEC. 7, 1941, THE TENNESSEE (BB34) WAS INBOARD OF THE WEST VIRGINIA, PRO-TECTED FROM TORPEDOES. BUT, WHEN THE WEST VIRGINIA SANK, SHE WEDGED THE TENNESSEE IN BETWEEN HERSELF AND THE QUAY. LATER, THE QUAY WAS BLOWN TO FREE THE TENNESSEE.

LATER, SHE GOT A NINE-MONTH REBUILD, EMERGING TOTALLY DIFFERENT.

IT CAN GET KIND'A LONESOME WHEN YOU DON'T SEE ANOTHER SHIP FOR WEEKS ON END. YOU FEEL LIKE YOU'RE ALL ALONE. OF COURSE, YOU'RE NOT, BUT DESTROYERS, WHEN OPERATING WITH OTHER SHIPS, ARE USUALLY IN THE VAN OR FAR ASEA OUT OF EYESIGHT OF OTHER SHIPS.

BECAUSE OF THIS, I WAS ALWAYS AMAZED AT THE GREAT NUMBER OF SHIPS I'D SEE IN THE HARBORS WHERE WE WOULD TAKE ON SUPPLIES OR "IRON UP" (TAKE ON AMMO).

EFATE WAS ONE SUCH HARBOR. TO ME, SEEING ALL THOSE SHIPS WAS A WELCOME SIGHT...SORT'A FAMILY.

HERE WE WOULD RELAX, MAKE KNIVES, GAME BOARDS, RINGS, CIGARETTE LIGHTERS, BELT BUCKLES, AND HOT PLATES, MUST'VE BEEN TWENTY OR SO HOT PLATES SCATTERED ABOUT OUR SHIP. WE MADE THEM OUT OF FIREBRICKS AND WIRE.

A FIREBRICK IS VERY LIGHT, EASY TO CUT OR GROOVE OUT...

WIRE WRAPPED AROUND A METAL ROD FORMED A COIL...

...WHICH WAS PLACED IN THE GROOVES TO SERVE AS A HEATING ELEMENT.

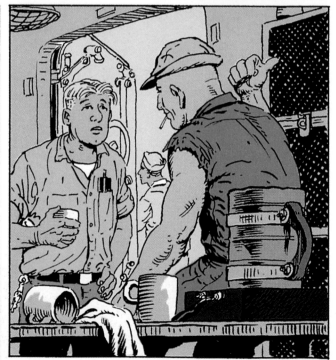

EVERY DIVISION HAD 'EM. THEY WERE IN SHAFT ALLEYS, FIRE AND ENGINE ROOMS, PAINT LOCKERS, SICK BAY, EVERYWHERE. COFFEE POTS WERE ALWAYS GOING. WITHOUT COFFEE, I DOUBT THAT SAILORS COULD EXIST.

SOMEWHERE ALONG THE LINE, JENKINS, OUR CHIEF ELECTRICIAN'S MATE, MADE WARRANT OFFICER. SOON'S HE BECAME AN OFFICER, HE BECAME A MARTINET. HE CONFISCATED ALL THE HOT PLATES. ONE NIGHT, THE SKIPPER ON THE BRIDGE...

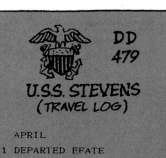

DD 479

U.S.S. STEVENS
(TRAVEL LOG)

APRIL
1 DEPARTED EFATE
2 ARRIVED ESPIRITU SANTO.
3 DEPARTED, ARRIVED EFATE.
7 DEPARTED, ARRIVED MILNE BAY, NEW GUINEA.
8 DEPARTED MILNE BAY FOR BUNA BAY, N.G.
18 LEFT BUNA BAY.
23 SUPPORTED LANDINGS AT TANAHMERAH, N.G.

GET ME A CUP OF COFFEE FROM THE SICK BAY *!

AIN'T NO COFFEE, CAPTAIN.

*THE SKIPPER ESPECIALLY LIKED THE SICK BAY COFFEE.

WHY, WHAT'S WRONG?

WE AIN'T GOT ANY HOT PLATES, CAPTAIN.

WHY?

JENKINS PICKED 'EM UP, SAID THEY WERE FIRE HAZARDS.

GET JENKINS UP HERE!

I UNDERSTAND YOU PICKED UP ALL THE HOT PLATES BECAUSE THEY WERE FIRE HAZARDS!

YESSIR!

WELL, THAT'S COMMENDABLE, YOU'RE RIGHT. TWO THINGS: YOU'RE THE ELECTRICAL OFFICER ON THIS SHIP, RIGHT?

YESSIR!

YOU KNOW A LOT ABOUT ELECTRICITY, RIGHT?

YESSIR!?

WELL, I WANT ALL THE HOT PLATES BACK IN PLACE. BUT FIRST YOU REWIRE AND FIREPROOF THEM!

YEP! SAILORS LIVED ON COFFEE, AN' OUR SKIPPER WAS A "REAL" SAILOR.

SPEAKING OF COFFEE...

SINCE OUR FORCES WERE LEAPFROGGING MANY JAPANESE-HELD ISLANDS...

THE DESPERATE ISLAND NATIVES STRANDED ON THESE BYPASSED ATOLLS WOULD WADE OUT, BRAVING SURF AND JAPANESE GUNFIRE, TO REACH THE SAFETY OF AMERICAN PTs* OR LCIs.

MANY DARING RESCUE MISSIONS WERE CARRIED OUT BY THESE SHALLOW DRAFT VESSELS.

*PATROL TORPEDO BOATS.

MOST OF THE EVACUATIONS WERE MET WITH STIFF JAPANESE RESISTANCE, YET OVER TWO THOUSAND NATIVES IN THE MARSHALLS ALONE WERE RESCUED.

WE TOOK OFF A BOATLOAD OF CIVILIANS FROM A PT ONCE TO TRANSFER 'EM TO AN LST. WHILE THEY WERE CLIMBING ABOARD OUR SHIP, THE CREW HANDED OUT BLANKETS, CLOTHES, AN' COFFEE. YOU GUESSED IT! THE NATIVES GRABBED THE COFFEE FIRST.

UNDERWAY WITH DESRON 25, THE STEVENS JOINED T/F77.4 OFF CAPE CRETIN AND SHAPED A COURSE FOR THE HOLLANDIA LANDINGS.

HERE OUR ECHELON DIVIDED. STEVENS SCREENED THE WESTERN GROUP WHILE ITS TROOPS LANDED AT TANA-MERAH BAY.

ABOUT THE ONLY THING THAT STICKS IN MY MIND ABOUT THE HOLLANDIA OPERATIONS IS THAT I MADE FIREMAN 1ST CLASS ON THAT DAY.

THE HOLLANDIA FORCES MOVED QUICKLY INLAND. ENCOUNTERING LIGHT RESISTANCE, THEY SECURED THREE AIRFIELDS WITHIN FIVE DAYS, QUELLING ALL OPPOSITION.

AND JOE KENNA, PULLING A BURNER BARREL, FORGOT TO SHUT OFF THE ROOT VALVE, I GOT SPRAYED WITH FUEL OIL. ALTHOUGH THE OIL WAS PREHEATED, IT WASN'T THAT HOT. BESIDES, SINCE I JUST MADE FIREMAN 1/C... IT WAS SORT'A LIKE A "BAPTISM."

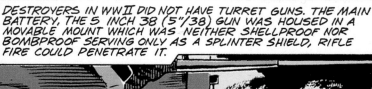

GUNS OF THE U.S.S. STEVENS (DD 479)

DD 479

U.S.S. STEVENS
(TRAVEL LOG)

MAY

2 ARRIVED BUNA, PATROL
   DUTY OFF CAPE CRETIN.

6 DEPARTED BUNA BAY.

10 ARRIVED PURVIS BAY,
   SOLOMONS.

12 DEPARTED PURVIS BAY.

13 ARRIVED NEW GEORGIA IS.

14-17 GUNNERY EXERCISES.

17 ARRIVED PURVIS BAY.

20 GUNNERY EX. GUADALCANAL.

31 ANTI SUB PATROL OFF
   GUADALCANAL.

DESTROYERS IN WW II DID NOT HAVE TURRET GUNS. THE MAIN BATTERY, THE 5 INCH 38 (5"/38) GUN WAS HOUSED IN A MOVABLE MOUNT WHICH WAS NEITHER SHELLPROOF NOR BOMBPROOF SERVING ONLY AS A SPLINTER SHIELD, RIFLE FIRE COULD PENETRATE IT.

A SEMI-AUTOMATIC GUN, IT WAS GOOD FOR ANTI-AIRCRAFT BARRAGE OR SALVOS AT SURFACE SHIPS AND SHORE BOMBARDMENTS. FIRING A 54 lb. PROJECTILE, IT COULD REACH AN AERIAL TARGET SIX MILES UP OR A SURFACE TARGET AT 18,000 YARDS. A GOOD GUN CREW COULD GET OFF 22 ROUNDS PER MINUTE,... AVERAGE WAS 15 RDS. IT FIRED SEMI-FIXED AMMUNITION. IN OTHER WORDS, THE ROUND WAS IN TWO PARTS: THE 54 lb. PROJECTILE AND A 28 lb. POWDER CASING.

BELOW THE GUN IN HANDLING ROOMS, SEAMEN SENT SHELLS AND POWDER UP TO THE GUN BY A POWER-DRIVEN HOIST EQUIPPED WITH AUTOMATIC FUSE-SETTING DEVICES.

THE GUNNERY OFFICER HEADED THREE DIVISIONS. THE MAIN BATTERIES WERE MANNED BY THE 1ST DIVISION. THE 40mm AND THE 20mm WERE MANNED BY THE 2ND DIVISION. THESE RATES WERE GUNNERS MATES (GM). THE 3RD DIVISION WERE THE FIRE CONTROL (FC) SONARMEN (SoM) AND TORPEDOMEN (TM).

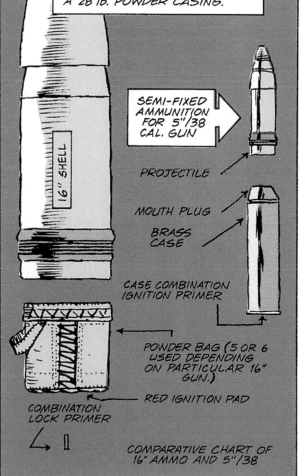

16" SHELL

SEMI-FIXED AMMUNITION FOR 5"/38 CAL. GUN

PROJECTILE

MOUTH PLUG

BRASS CASE

CASE COMBINATION IGNITION PRIMER

POWDER BAG (5 OR 6 USED DEPENDING ON PARTICULAR 16" GUN.)

RED IGNITION PAD

COMBINATION LOCK PRIMER

COMPARATIVE CHART OF 16" AMMO AND 5"/38

THE FIRE-CONTROL SYSTEM WHICH BASICALLY CONTROLS THE FIRING AND AIMING OF THE 5"/38 IS QUITE COMPLICATED. BRIEFLY... THE DIRECTOR ABOVE THE SHIP'S BRIDGE LOCATED THE TARGET. COMPUTERS LINKED TO IT AUTOMATICALLY TRANSMITTED SIGNALS TO POSITION (AIM) THE GUN. A GYROSCOPIC STABLE ELEMENT CORRECTED FOR PITCH AND ROLL. RANGE AND LINE-OF-SIGHT WAS TRANSMITTED TO A PLOTTING ROOM WHERE SPEED AND DIRECTION OF SHIP, PROBABLE SPEED OF TARGET, ANGLE, BALLISTICS AND WEATHER FACTORS WERE COMPUTED. THROUGH ELECTRICAL LINES AND SYNCHRO-ELECTRIC MOTORS, GUN ORDERS WERE THEN SENT TO INDICATORS, BY COMPUTER, AT THE DIFFERENT GUN MOUNTS. UNDER AUTOMATIC FIRE-CONTROL, THE FIRING OF THE GUNS, TRAIN AND ELEVATION, FUSE SETTING, TYPES OF AMMO, ETC., ETC., WAS ALL DONE BY REMOTE CONTROL... ALL THE GUN CREW HAD TO DO WAS LOAD THE GUNS. A BACK-UP SYSTEM PROVIDED FOR MANUAL CONTROL.

GM   FC   SoM   TM

SPECIALTY MARKS

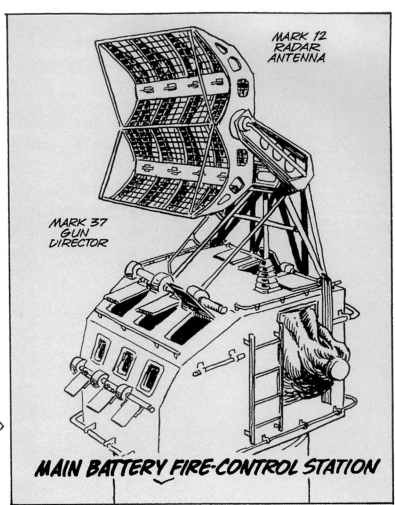

MARK 12 RADAR ANTENNA

MARK 37 GUN DIRECTOR

MAIN BATTERY FIRE-CONTROL STATION

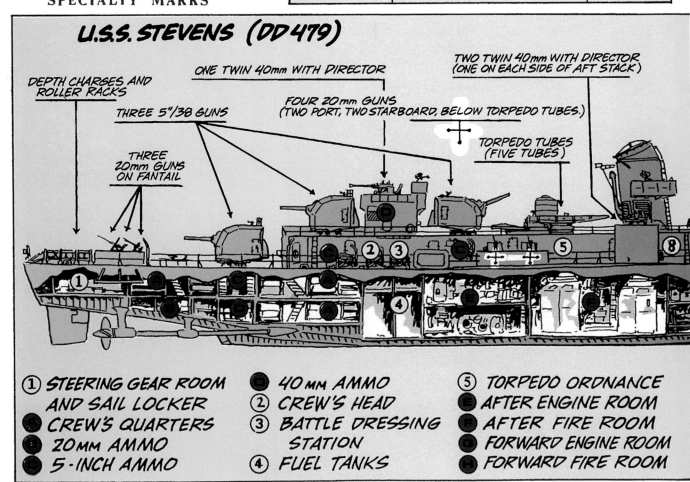

U.S.S. STEVENS (DD 479)

ONE TWIN 40mm WITH DIRECTOR

TWO TWIN 40mm WITH DIRECTOR (ONE ON EACH SIDE OF AFT STACK)

DEPTH CHARGES AND ROLLER RACKS

THREE 5"/38 GUNS

FOUR 20mm GUNS (TWO PORT, TWO STARBOARD, BELOW TORPEDO TUBES.)

THREE 20mm GUNS ON FANTAIL

TORPEDO TUBES (FIVE TUBES)

① STEERING GEAR ROOM AND SAIL LOCKER
Ⓐ CREW'S QUARTERS
Ⓑ 20mm AMMO
Ⓒ 5-INCH AMMO

Ⓓ 40mm AMMO
② CREW'S HEAD
③ BATTLE DRESSING STATION
④ FUEL TANKS

⑤ TORPEDO ORDNANCE
Ⓔ AFTER ENGINE ROOM
Ⓕ AFTER FIRE ROOM
Ⓖ FORWARD ENGINE ROOM
Ⓗ FORWARD FIRE ROOM

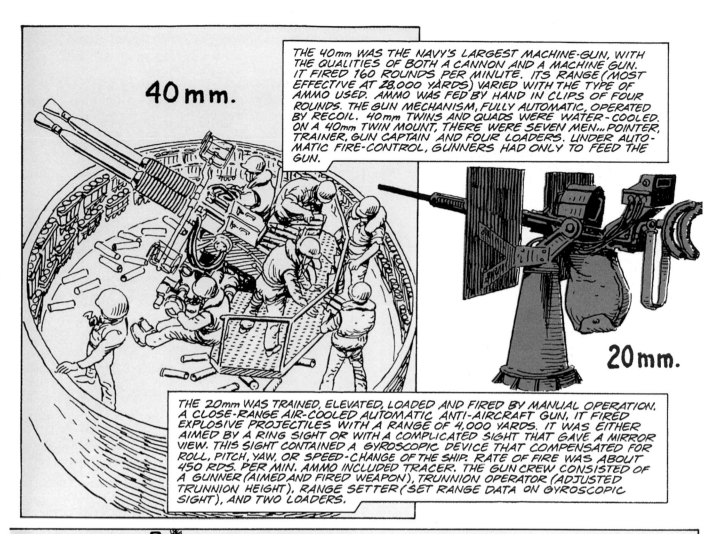

40mm.

THE 40mm WAS THE NAVY'S LARGEST MACHINE-GUN, WITH THE QUALITIES OF BOTH A CANNON AND A MACHINE-GUN. IT FIRED 160 ROUNDS PER MINUTE. ITS RANGE (MOST EFFECTIVE AT 28,000 YARDS) VARIED WITH THE TYPE OF AMMO USED. AMMO WAS FED BY HAND IN CLIPS OF FOUR ROUNDS. THE GUN MECHANISM, FULLY AUTOMATIC, OPERATED BY RECOIL. 40mm TWINS AND QUADS WERE WATER-COOLED. ON A 40mm TWIN MOUNT, THERE WERE SEVEN MEN... POINTER, TRAINER, GUN CAPTAIN AND FOUR LOADERS. UNDER AUTO-MATIC FIRE-CONTROL, GUNNERS HAD ONLY TO FEED THE GUN.

20mm.

THE 20mm WAS TRAINED, ELEVATED, LOADED AND FIRED BY MANUAL OPERATION. A CLOSE-RANGE AIR-COOLED AUTOMATIC ANTI-AIRCRAFT GUN, IT FIRED EXPLOSIVE PROJECTILES WITH A RANGE OF 4,000 YARDS. IT WAS EITHER AIMED BY A RING SIGHT OR WITH A COMPLICATED SIGHT THAT GAVE A MIRROR VIEW. THIS SIGHT CONTAINED A GYROSCOPIC DEVICE THAT COMPENSATED FOR ROLL, PITCH, YAW, OR SPEED-CHANGE OF THE SHIP. RATE OF FIRE WAS ABOUT 450 RDS. PER MIN. AMMO INCLUDED TRACER. THE GUN CREW CONSISTED OF A GUNNER (AIMED AND FIRED WEAPON), TRUNNION OPERATOR (ADJUSTED TRUNNION HEIGHT), RANGE SETTER (SET RANGE DATA ON GYROSCOPIC SIGHT), AND TWO LOADERS.

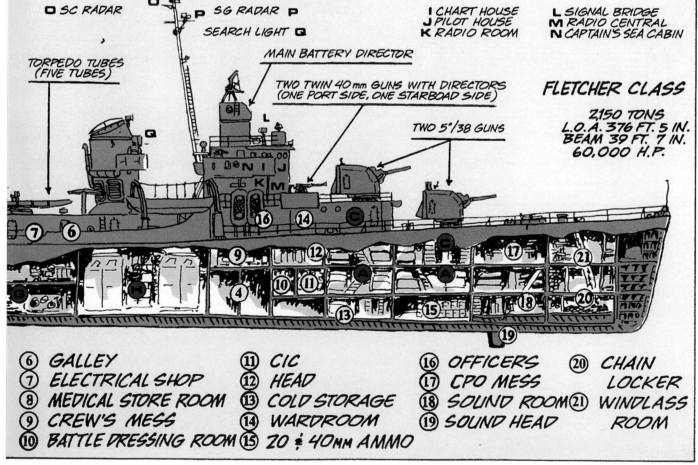

O SC RADAR
P SG RADAR
Q SEARCH LIGHT

I CHART HOUSE
J PILOT HOUSE
K RADIO ROOM

L SIGNAL BRIDGE
M RADIO CENTRAL
N CAPTAIN'S SEA CABIN

TORPEDO TUBES
(FIVE TUBES)

MAIN BATTERY DIRECTOR

TWO TWIN 40mm GUNS WITH DIRECTORS
(ONE PORT SIDE, ONE STARBOAD SIDE)

TWO 5"/38 GUNS

FLETCHER CLASS

2,150 TONS
L.O.A. 376 FT. 5 IN.
BEAM 39 FT. 7 IN.
60,000 H.P.

⑥ GALLEY
⑦ ELECTRICAL SHOP
⑧ MEDICAL STORE ROOM
⑨ CREW'S MESS
⑩ BATTLE DRESSING ROOM

⑪ CIC
⑫ HEAD
⑬ COLD STORAGE
⑭ WARDROOM
⑮ 20 & 40mm AMMO

⑯ OFFICERS
⑰ CPO MESS
⑱ SOUND ROOM
⑲ SOUND HEAD

⑳ CHAIN
    LOCKER
㉑ WINDLASS
    ROOM

U.S.S. STEVENS
(TRAVEL LOG)

DD 479

JUNE

4 DEPARTED GUADALCANAL.

8 ARRIVED KWAJALEIN.

10 DEPARTED.

11 ARRIVED ENIWETOK ATOLL.

12 DEPARTED.

13 ORDERS TO GUAM CHANGED TO STAND BY SAIPAN.

28 DEPARTED.

28 ARRIVED ENIWETOK.

ONCE MORE, I TRIED SLEEPING TOPSIDE, THIS TIME, UP ON THE STACK, LASHING MY HAMMOCK TO THE SEARCHLIGHT PLATFORM.

I FORGOT ABOUT THE FIREROOMS BLOWING TUBES.!

BLOW TUBES.!!

PHOOOMM

THIS WAS DONE TO KEEP THE TUBES AND FIREBOXES AS CLEAN AS POSSIBLE. BLOWERS ARE TURNED UP FULL BLAST. SOOT, SCALE, AND OTHER DEPOSITS ARE BLASTED OFF AND SENT SPEWING OUT OF THE STACK. IT IS DONE AT NIGHT TO AVOID ENEMY DETECTION.

ATTACHED TO THE 5TH FLEET, WE JOINED TF58 FOR THE INVASION OF THE MARIANAS (CODE NAME "FORAGER").

DD 479
U.S.S. STEVENS
(TRAVEL LOG)

JULY
10- 11 PATROL DUTY OFF EN
IWETOK.
14- 15 PATROL DUTY.
17 DEPARTED AREA.
22- 24 ENGAGED IN BOMBARD-
MENT AND SUPPORTED
LANDINGS ON GUAM.
25 DEPARTED AREA.
30 ARRIVED ENIWETOK.
31 DEPARTED AREA.

COMING UP FROM WATCH ONE DAY, I WAS SURPRISED TO SEE A MOB BACK AFT, MOSTLY GUNNERS AND OFFICERS.

THEY WERE HAVING SOME KIND OF POW-WOW AND WERE STUDYING A FANTASTIC THREE-DIMENSIONAL MAP OF GUAM. EVERYTHING, FROM AIRFIELDS TO LATRINES, WAS ON IT. THESE MODELS, DEVEL-OPED BY THE HYDROGRAPHIC OFFICE OF THE NAVY IN COOPER-ATION WITH THE BUREAU OF AERONAUTICS, WERE ALREADY IN USE BY PILOTS, BUT IT WAS SOMETHING NEW FOR THE FLEET SHIPS.

THE NAMES OF SPORTS AND SPORTING EQUIPMENT WERE USED AS CODE NAMES FOR THE MANY TARGETS.

WE HAD THE DUBIOUS HONOR OF KNOCKING OUT THE LATRINES. CODE NAME "HOCKEY PUCK." CRIPES! WE WERE CRESTFALLEN. CAN YOU IMAGINE? AFTER COUNTLESS BOMBARDMENTS, AIR ATTACKS AND 3 STAR AWARDS TO OUR CREDIT -- LATRINES ??

WELL, WE SHELLED THEM @%!☆# "HOCKEY PUCKS," WE HIT THEM WITH HARASSING FIRE, CALL FIRE, AND ILLUMIN-ATION. THIS WAS STEADY, CONTINUOUS FIRING, THREE DAYS, I THINK. I REMEMBER WE ATE AT OUR GUNS.

ALSO, IT SEEMED, ENEMY AIR RESISTANCE WAS LIGHT. THE JAPANESE DIVE BOMBERS WERE IN THE AIR, BUT NOT VERY MANY OF THEM -- WHAT IS NOW KNOWN AS "THE MARIANAS TURKEY SHOOT" ATTRIBUTED TO THIS.

THE TROOPERS WERE HITTING THE BEACHES. I REMEMBER SEEING THE RETURNING CASUALTIES. BOATLOAD UPON BOATLOAD, THEY SCUDDED PAST US IN A MEL-ANCHOLY STREAM HEADED FOR THE HOSPITAL SHIP.

AS I WATCHED THE "BATTLEWAGONS" FIRE, IT SEEMED TO ME THEIR 16 INCH SHELLS HAD MINIMAL EFFECT, COMPARED TO THE STEVENS' HITS WITH HER LITTLE 5 INCHERS.

I COULDN'T FIGURE IT OUT. I WAS AWED BY THE POWER OF OUR GUNS. DID WE HAVE SOME KIND OF SOUPED UP SHELLS ?? NO WAY.!!

THE JAPANESE BELIEVED THAT THE U.S. NAVY WOULD NEVER WASTE SHELLS ON LATRINES, AND HAD SWITCHED THINGS AROUND. THEY HAD PLACED AMMO AROUND THE LATRINES. WE WERE HITTING AMMO DUMPS!

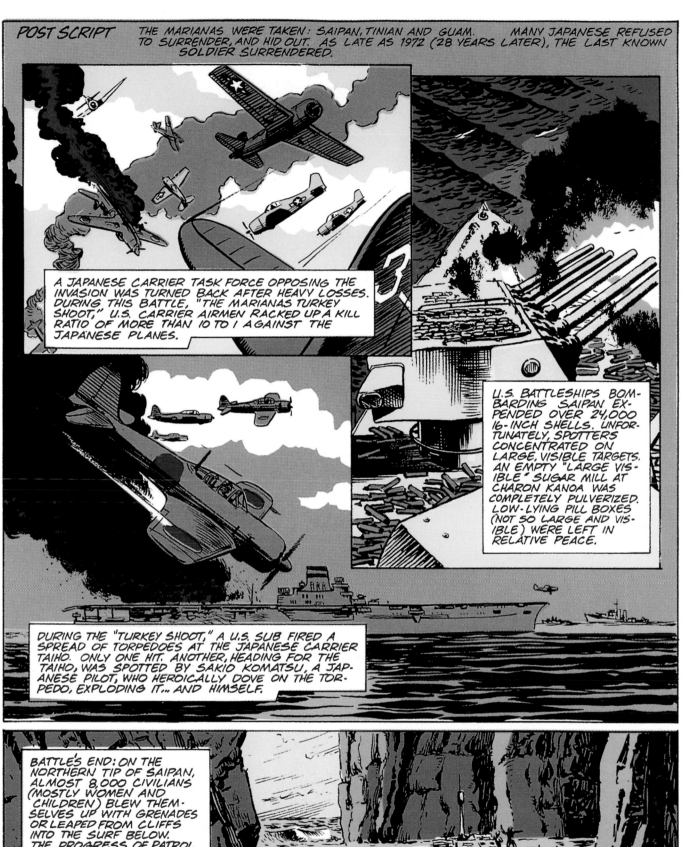

POST SCRIPT THE MARIANAS WERE TAKEN: SAIPAN, TINIAN AND GUAM.   MANY JAPANESE REFUSED TO SURRENDER, AND HID OUT. AS LATE AS 1972 (28 YEARS LATER), THE LAST KNOWN SOLDIER SURRENDERED.

A JAPANESE CARRIER TASK FORCE OPPOSING THE INVASION WAS TURNED BACK AFTER HEAVY LOSSES. DURING THIS BATTLE, "THE MARIANAS TURKEY SHOOT," U.S. CARRIER AIRMEN RACKED UP A KILL RATIO OF MORE THAN 10 TO 1 AGAINST THE JAPANESE PLANES.

U.S. BATTLESHIPS BOM-BARDING SAIPAN EX-PENDED OVER 24,000 16-INCH SHELLS. UNFOR-TUNATELY, SPOTTERS CONCENTRATED ON LARGE, VISIBLE TARGETS. AN EMPTY "LARGE VIS-IBLE" SUGAR MILL AT CHARON KANOA WAS COMPLETELY PULVERIZED. LOW-LYING PILL BOXES (NOT SO LARGE AND VIS-IBLE) WERE LEFT IN RELATIVE PEACE.

DURING THE "TURKEY SHOOT," A U.S. SUB FIRED A SPREAD OF TORPEDOES AT THE JAPANESE CARRIER TAIHO. ONLY ONE HIT. ANOTHER, HEADING FOR THE TAIHO, WAS SPOTTED BY SAKIO KOMATSU, A JAP-ANESE PILOT, WHO HEROICALLY DOVE ON THE TOR-PEDO, EXPLODING IT... AND HIMSELF.

BATTLE'S END: ON THE NORTHERN TIP OF SAIPAN, ALMOST 8,000 CIVILIANS (MOSTLY WOMEN AND CHILDREN) BLEW THEM-SELVES UP WITH GRENADES OR LEAPED FROM CLIFFS INTO THE SURF BELOW. THE PROGRESS OF PATROL BOATS THROUGH HUNDREDS OF TORN AND BLOATED BODIES WAS SLOW, TEDIOUS, AND HEART-RENDING.

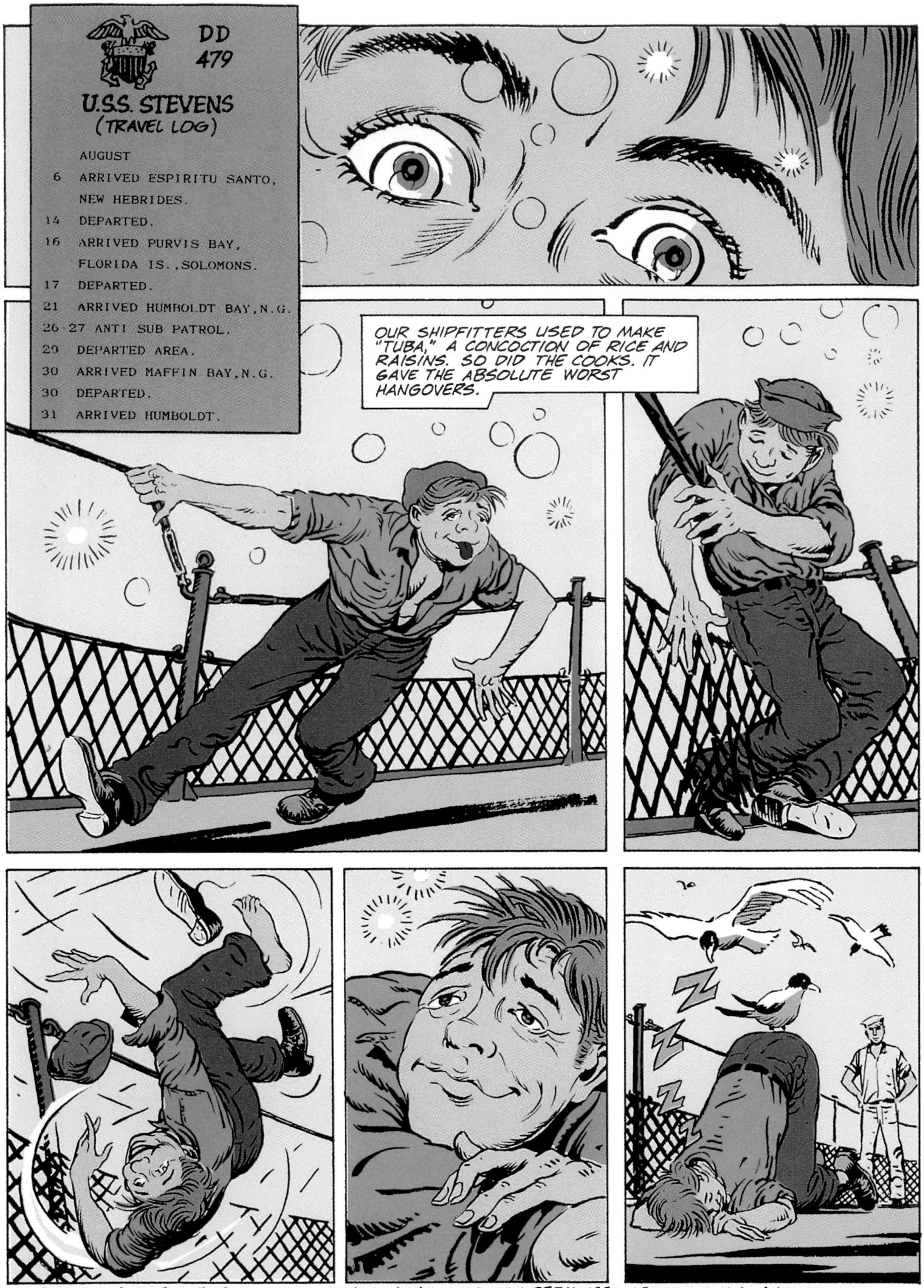
DD 479
U.S.S. STEVENS
(TRAVEL LOG)
AUGUST
6 ARRIVED ESPIRITU SANTO, NEW HEBRIDES.
14 DEPARTED.
16 ARRIVED PURVIS BAY, FLORIDA IS., SOLOMONS.
17 DEPARTED.
21 ARRIVED HUMBOLDT BAY, N.G.
26-27 ANTI SUB PATROL.
29 DEPARTED AREA.
30 ARRIVED MAFFIN BAY, N.G.
30 DEPARTED.
31 ARRIVED HUMBOLDT.
OUR SHIPFITTERS USED TO MAKE "TUBA," A CONCOCTION OF RICE AND RAISINS. SO DID THE COOKS. IT GAVE THE ABSOLUTE WORST HANGOVERS.
Z Z Z

THE ABOVE IS AN EXTREME EXAGGERATION. ALCOHOL WAS NOT PERMITTED ABOARD A U.S. SHIP OF WAR. ANYONE FOUND WITH IT, OR IN AN INTOXICATED STATE, WOULD HAVE BEEN IN SERIOUS TROUBLE.

DD 479

U.S.S. STEVENS
(TRAVEL LOG)

SEPTEMBER

1- 6 PATROL DUTY.
7 DEPARTED AREA.
8 ARRIVED AITAPE, N.G.
10 DEPARTED AREA.
15 BOMBARDED MOROTAI.
16 DEPARTED AREA.
18 ARRIVED HUMBOLDT BAY, N.G.
19 DEPARTED AREA.
23 ARRIVED MOROTAI.
24-28 PATROL PASSAGE BE- TWEEN HALMAHERA AND MOROTAI.
28 DEPARTED.

WHILE BOMBARDING MOROTAI AND SUPPORTING THE ASSAULT TROOPS, WE SHOT DOWN OUR FIRST "JUDY." IN THE MONTHS TO FOLLOW, WE WOULD BE SEEING A LOT OF HER KIND.

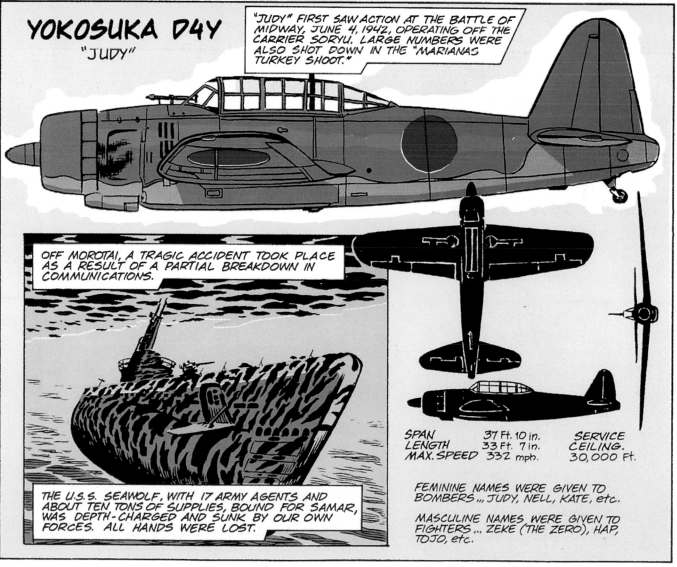

YOKOSUKA D4Y
"JUDY"

"JUDY" FIRST SAW ACTION AT THE BATTLE OF MIDWAY, JUNE 4, 1942, OPERATING OFF THE CARRIER SORYU. LARGE NUMBERS WERE ALSO SHOT DOWN IN THE "MARIANAS TURKEY SHOOT."

OFF MOROTAI, A TRAGIC ACCIDENT TOOK PLACE AS A RESULT OF A PARTIAL BREAKDOWN IN COMMUNICATIONS.

SPAN	37 Ft. 10 in.	SERVICE	
LENGTH	33 Ft. 7 in.	CEILING.	
MAX. SPEED	332 mph.	30,000 Ft.	

THE U.S.S. SEAWOLF, WITH 17 ARMY AGENTS AND ABOUT TEN TONS OF SUPPLIES, BOUND FOR SAMAR, WAS DEPTH-CHARGED AND SUNK BY OUR OWN FORCES. ALL HANDS WERE LOST.

FEMININE NAMES WERE GIVEN TO BOMBERS ... JUDY, NELL, KATE, etc.

MASCULINE NAMES WERE GIVEN TO FIGHTERS ... ZEKE (THE ZERO), HAP, TOJO, etc.

DD
479

U.S.S. STEVENS
(TRAVEL LOG)

OCTOBER

4 ARRIVED HUMBOLDT.

16 DEPARTED AREA.

22 BOMBARDED AND SUPPORTED
    LANDINGS AT LEYTE, P.I.

22 DEPARTED.

28 ARRIVED HUMBOLDT.

30 DEPARTED.

AT THE BATTLE OF LEYTE GULF, THINGS REALLY HEATED UP. NEARLY EVERY TYPE OF VESSEL-- SUBMARINES, PT BOATS, CRUISERS AND DESTROYERS--WERE IN THIS FREE-FOR-ALL. HERE THE LAST BATTLESHIP VS. BATTLESHIP, THE LAST CARRIER VS. CARRIER BATTLE WAS FOUGHT. WHEN IT ENDED, THE JAPANESE NAVY AS A FIGHTING FORCE WAS JUST ABOUT FINISHED.

IT WAS HERE ALSO THAT FOR THE FIRST TIME THE JAPANESE SUICIDE PILOTS, THE KAMIKAZE, MADE THEIR "DEBUT."

THEY WERE LIKE DRAGONS.

THEY SEEMED TO MATERIALIZE EVERYWHERE.

ALL WE COULD DO WAS SHOOT FASTER AND KEEP SHOOTING.

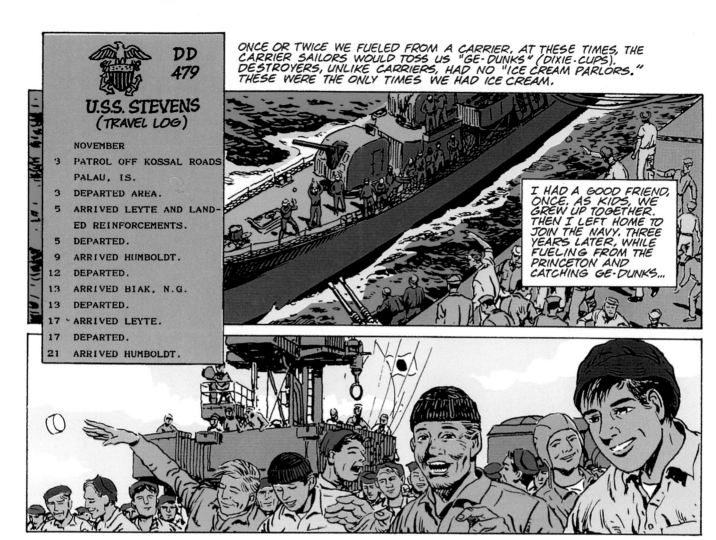

DD 479

U.S.S. STEVENS
(TRAVEL LOG)

NOVEMBER
3 PATROL OFF KOSSAL ROADS PALAU, IS.
3 DEPARTED AREA.
5 ARRIVED LEYTE AND LAND-ED REINFORCEMENTS.
5 DEPARTED.
9 ARRIVED HUMBOLDT.
12 DEPARTED.
13 ARRIVED BIAK, N.G.
13 DEPARTED.
17 ARRIVED LEYTE.
17 DEPARTED.
21 ARRIVED HUMBOLDT.

ONCE OR TWICE WE FUELED FROM A CARRIER. AT THESE TIMES, THE CARRIER SAILORS WOULD TOSS US "GE-DUNKS" (DIXIE-CUPS). DESTROYERS, UNLIKE CARRIERS, HAD NO "ICE CREAM PARLORS." THESE WERE THE ONLY TIMES WE HAD ICE CREAM.

I HAD A GOOD FRIEND, ONCE. AS KIDS, WE GREW UP TOGETHER. THEN I LEFT HOME TO JOIN THE NAVY. THREE YEARS LATER, WHILE FUELING FROM THE PRINCETON AND CATCHING GE-DUNKS...

... A STRANGE AND MYSTERIOUS THING HAPPENED. A COMPELLING FORCE CAUSED ME TO LOOK INTO THE EYES OF A SAILOR ON THE CARRIER'S FLIGHT DECK. AMIDST HUNDREDS OF GUYS, HUNDREDS OF FEET APART, OUR EYES MET. MINE ALMOST POPPED OUT 'A THEIR SOCKETS.' IT WAS HIM !!! MY FRIEND.' THE REALLY STRANGE PART ABOUT IT WAS THAT I DIDN'T EVEN **KNOW** HE WAS IN THE SERVICE SINCE WE HADN'T KEPT IN TOUCH. WE WEREN'T WITHIN SHOUTING DISTANCE SO HAD WE NOT LOCKED EYES AT THAT VERY INSTANT, WE WOULD NEVER HAVE KNOWN OF THAT MEETING.'

AS I RAN TO OUR SIGNAL BRIDGE, I SAW HIM TAKE OFF, TOO. WE WERE ABOUT TO GET OUR SIGNALMEN TO "TALK" BETWEEN SHIPS FOR US. BUT, BEFORE WE COULD, OUR SHIPS PARTED. WELL, THERE HAD BEEN TIMES BEFORE AT EFATE, NOUMEA, AND MILNE BAY, WHERE OUR SHIPS HAD BEEN IN PORT TOGETHER. NEXT TIME, WE'D VISIT.

BUT, NO.' A FEW DAYS LATER, OFF THE PHILIPPINES, HIS CARRIER WAS SUNK... GOODBYE, OLD FRIEND.

WHAT THE JAPANESE FAILED TO DO TO OUR FLEET, THE WEATHER DID FOR THEM. ON DEC. 17TH, A TYPHOON HIT TF38. IT RIPPED THROUGH US LIKE A VACUUM CLEANER.

DD 479

U.S.S. STEVENS
(TRAVEL LOG)

DECEMBER
3   DEPARTED HUMBOLDT.
8   ARRIVED LEYTE, P.I.
12 DEPARTED.
15 ARRIVED MINDORO, IS.
15 DEPARTED.
18 ARRIVED LEYTE.
20 23 PATROL OFF SAMAR IS.
     PHILIPPINES.
27 DEPARTED.

800 SAILORS LOST THEIR LIVES IN THAT SCREAMING NIGHTMARE. 3 DESTROYERS WENT DOWN, 20 SHIPS WERE DAMAGED, AND 146 AIRCRAFT WERE DESTROYED.

OUR SHIP WAS A' ROCKIN' AN' A' ROLLIN', A' PITCHIN' AN' A' PUMPIN'. ONCE SHE TOOK A 50° ROLL AN' JUST LAID THERE LIKE A DEAD DOG. IT SEEMED FOREVER BEFORE SHE RIGHTED HERSELF... YOU NEVER HEARD SO MUCH PRAYING IN YOUR LIFE.

ONLY ABOUT SEVEN GUYS SHOWED UP FOR CHOW THAT DAY.

YEAH, WE HAD CHOW. FRANKS, BEANS, AND SAUERKRAUT WERE ON THE MENU.

IN JANUARY OF 1945, WE WERE IN AN' OUT, UP AN' DOWN, AN' ALL AROUND LEYTE GULF, CONVOYING TROOPS AND SUPPLIES.

DD 479

U.S.S. STEVENS
(TRAVEL LOG)

JANUARY 1945
1   ROUND TRIP TO MINDORO.
6   DEPARTED LEYTE.
13 ARRIVED LINGAYEN GULF.
    LUZON, P.I.
14- 18 PATROL AND PICKET
    DUTY.
18 DEPARTED.
23 ARRIVED LEYTE.

CONVOYS CAN BECOME KIND'A MONOTONOUS... SOMETIMES.

I HAD COME UP FOR SOME SUNSHINE. WHILE I WAS SHOOTING THE BREEZE WITH PINKY AND OX, I HAPPENED TO THINK OF A QUESTION I WAS ASKED ONCE, ABOUT WHAT KIND OF UNIFORMS WE WORE ABOARD SHIP. I STARTED TO LAUGH.

WHAT'S SO FUNNY?

YEAH, SAM! YOU GOT A NEW JOKE?

Nah! JUST LOOKIN' AT OUR "UNIFORMS." THE ONLY THING UNIFORM ABOUT US GUYS IS OUR HATS, AND EVEN WITH THAT, EVERYONE HAS HIS OWN STYLE. HA! AND THEM OLD SHOES YOU CUT OPEN FOR SANDALS!! SOME UNIFORMS WE GOT!

OX WENT BACK AFT TO "BEND" A LINE TO NEW DUNGAREES. TOWING THEM THROUGH THE SALT WATER A COUPL'A HOURS WOULD SOFTEN 'EM UP.

I WENT BELOW FOR COFFEE. PINKY WATCHED THE FLYING FISH RACE OUR SHIP. CONVOYS CAN BE KIND'A MONOTONOUS...

MAN YOUR BATTLE STATIONS!!

...SOMETIMES.

ON THIS CONVOY, WE RACKED UP A FAIR SCORE: 2 TWIN ENGINE BOMBERS, A TOJO, AND A JUDY.

THE FIRST BOMBER GOT THROUGH OUR 5-INCH BURST, BUT OUR SECONDARY GUNNERS POSITIVELY RIDDLED THE PLANE. WITHOUT A DOUBT THEY PERFORATED THE PILOT. THEN, AN EXPLOSION.

THE TOJO WAS UP HIGH, DANCING AROUND AS IF TRYING TO DECIDE HOW TO COME DOWN...IN A STEEP DIVE, AN ANGLE, WHAT? PROXIMITY BURSTS AND DIRECT HITS "DECIDED" FOR HIM. HE CAME DOWN...IN A BALL OF FIRE.

LATER "HELEN" AND "JUDY" PAID US A VISIT. I'D BEEN ON BLIND DATES BEFORE, BUT THIS WAS THE UGLIEST PAIR I EVER HOPE TO MEET. "HELEN" WAS GREETED BY A SHOWER OF SALVOS, AND SLOPPED OVER. SHE MADE A SHALLOW DIVE, THEN RUSHED IN WITH THE VELOCITY OF A COMET... AND WAS PROMPTLY SHREDDED.

"JUDY" WAS WELCOMED WITH A SHELL THAT PASSED RIGHT THROUGH HER, SOMEHOW NOT EXPLODING. OR, MAYBE IT WAS A LARGE PIECE OF SHRAPNEL--ANYWAY, IT SPLIT HER OPEN LIKE A MELON. THEN FIRE BEGAN TO VOMIT FROM HER COCKPIT.

BUT SHE KEPT COMING. FRAGMENTS, PIECES WERE SHOWERING FROM HER, WHEN SUDDENLY REDUCED TO SCRAP, SHE JUST TOPPLED OVER LIKE A CHOPPED PINE TREE AND FELL INTO THE SEA.

AN LCI HAD BEEN HIT. I COULD SEE BODIES AND BODY PARTS ALL OVER.

OUR SKIPPER SENT OUR WHALEBOAT OUT WITH MULLIGAN, OUR PhM.* TO HELP.

*PHARMACIST'S MATE.

SINCE THE LCI DIDN'T HAVE THE PROPER MEDICAL FACILITIES ABOARD, MULLIGAN TOOK ONE GUY WHO WAS ESPECIALLY BANGED UP TO A CRUISER (THEY HAD GOOD OPERATING ROOMS).

BUT, FOR REASONS UNKNOWN TO ME, THEY REFUSED TO HELP. MULLIGAN, CUSSIN' THE CRUISER, BROUGHT THE WOUNDED BOY TO OUR SHIP.

MULLIGAN, WHO WAS ONLY A PhM, DID A GOOD JOB.
LEASTWAYS, NO COMPLAINTS FROM HIS PATIENT.

WE HAD BEEN IN THE PACIFIC FOR ABOUT 14 MONTHS STRAIGHT ON THIS, OUR SECOND VOYAGE. LIBERTY? IT WAS LITERALLY, THE FEW TIMES WE HAD IT, NOTHING BUT GOING ASHORE ON SOME REMOTE JUNGLE ISLAND, DRINKING OUR TWO OR THREE ALLOTTED BOTTLES OF BEER, AND RETURNING TO OUR SHIP. AT THE TIME, I KEPT A SKETCH BOOK (OF SORTS). BELOW ARE SCENES FROM TWO SUCH LIBERTIES AND A FEW GAGS MADE FOR MY SHIPMATES.

DD 479

U.S.S. STEVENS
(TRAVEL LOG)

FEBRUARY
2 DEPARTED LEYTE.
3-5 PATROL.
9 ARRIVED LINGAYEN GULF, LUZON, PHILIPPINE ISLANDS
10 DEPARTED.
13 ARRIVED LEYTE.
13 DEPARTED.
18 ARRIVED MANUS ISLAND, ADMIRALTY ISLANDS.
24 DEPARTED.
25 ARRIVED HUMBOLDT BAY, N.G.
28 DEPARTED NEW GUINEA.

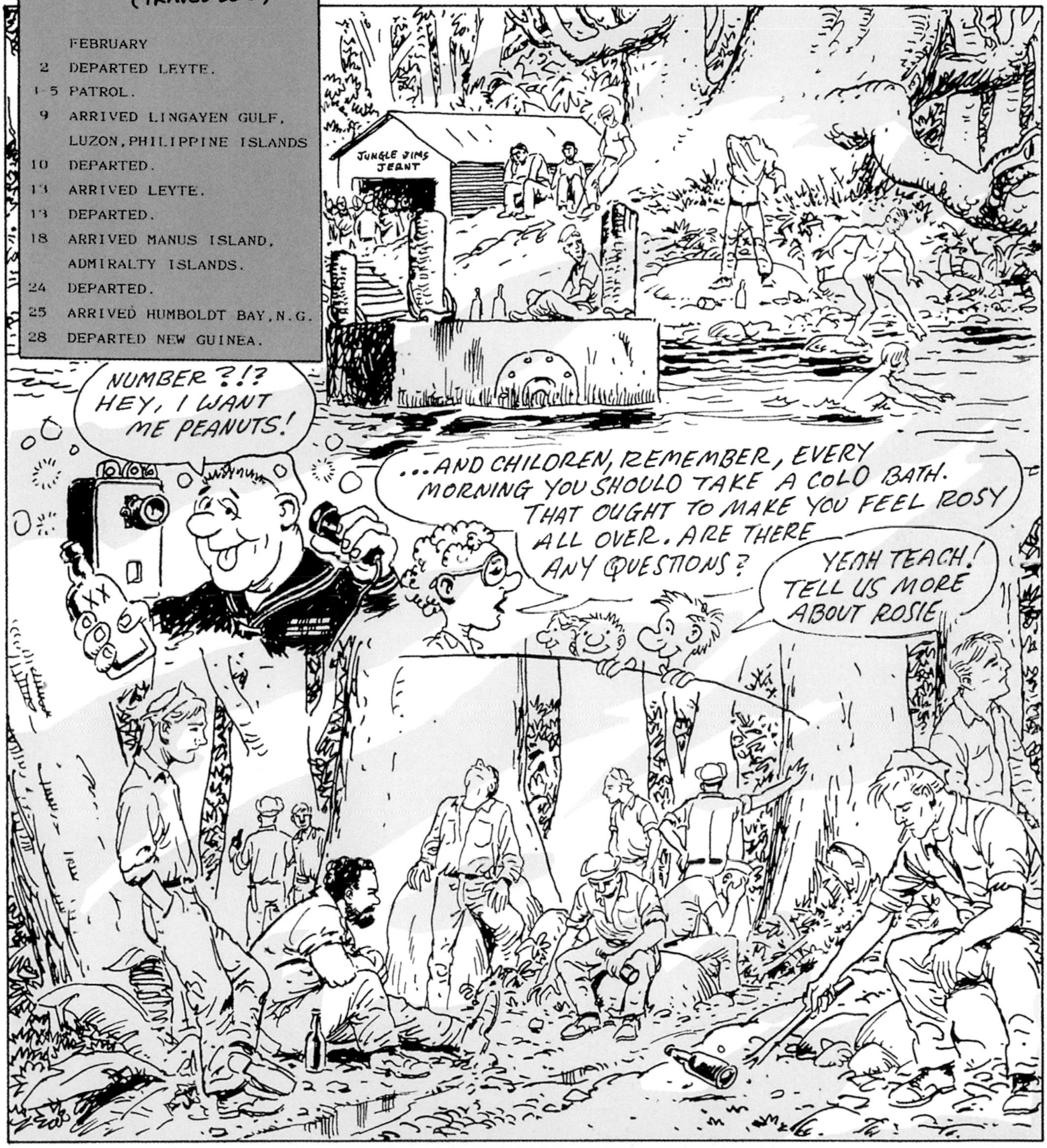
JUNGLE JIMS JERNT
NUMBER ?!? HEY, I WANT ME PEANUTS!
...AND CHILDREN, REMEMBER, EVERY MORNING YOU SHOULD TAKE A COLD BATH. THAT OUGHT TO MAKE YOU FEEL ROSY ALL OVER. ARE THERE ANY QUESTIONS?
YEAH TEACH! TELL US MORE ABOUT ROSIE

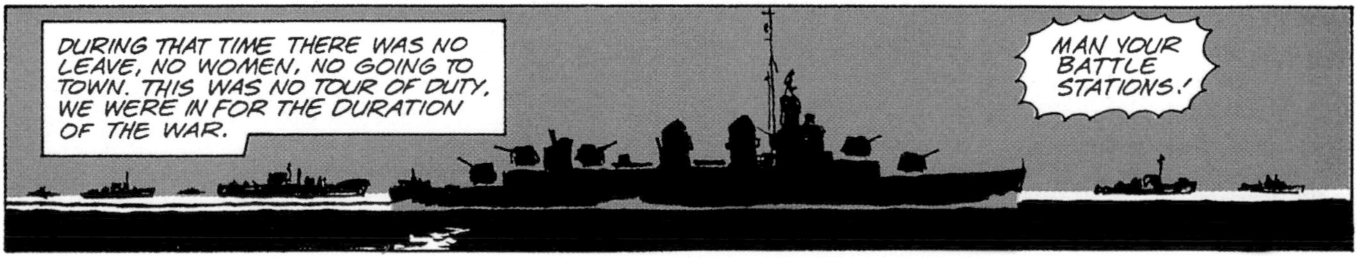
DURING THAT TIME THERE WAS NO LEAVE, NO WOMEN, NO GOING TO TOWN. THIS WAS NO TOUR OF DUTY. WE WERE IN FOR THE DURATION OF THE WAR.
MAN YOUR BATTLE STATIONS!

THE DARKEST NIGHT NEVER HID THE HORROR. THE MOST BEAUTIFUL DAY NEVER STOPPED THE SLAUGHTER. AND TIME WAS BEGINNING TO ERODE OUR DREAMS.

WHILE STEAMING WITH THE 7ᵀᴴ FLEET, THE STEVENS AND ANOTHER DESTROYER WERE CALLED OUT TO SEARCH FOR SURVIVORS OF A DOWNED B-24 BOMBER.

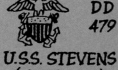

DD 479

U.S.S. STEVENS
(TRAVEL LOG)

MARCH
6   ARRIVED MANILA.
6   DEPARTED.
6   ARRIVED SUBIC BAY, P.I.
9   DEPARTED.
10 ARRIVED MINDORO FOR
    PATROL. 11 DEPARTED.
12 ARRIVED LINGAYEN GULF
13 DEPARTED LINGAYEN. OUT
    INTO CHINA SEA IN
    SEARCH FOR BOMBER CREW
16 ARRIVED MINDORO.
17 DEPARTED.
18 ARRIVED PANAY IS. AND
    SUPPORTED LANDINGS.
18-20 PATROL OFF PANAY.
20 DEPARTED.
21 ARRIVED SUBIC BAY.

SIX MEN WERE FOUND.

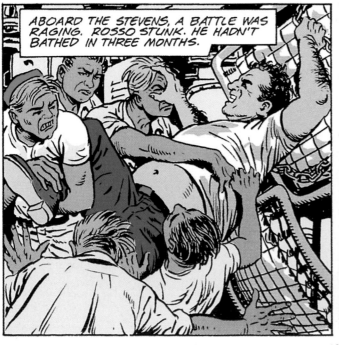

ABOARD THE STEVENS, A BATTLE WAS RAGING. ROSSO STUNK. HE HADN'T BATHED IN THREE MONTHS.

WE GOT HIM UNDER A SHOWER AND KI-YI'D * HIM, CLOTHES AND ALL.

*KI-YI: A VERY COARSE SCRUB BRUSH. CAN TAKE THE HIDE OFF YOU.

ON APRIL 1ST, 1945, AFTER FIVE DAYS OF SHIP BOMBARDMENT AND AERIAL BOMBINGS, THE U.S. ASSAULTED THE SIXTY-MILE BANANA-SHAPED ISLAND OF OKINAWA.

MEANWHILE, JAPAN HAD MANAGED TO GATHER TOGETHER A SIZEABLE FLEET WHICH WAS APPROACHING THE ISLAND TO OPPOSE THE LANDINGS.

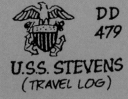

DD 479

U.S.S. STEVENS
(TRAVEL LOG)

APRIL
3   DEPARTED SUBIC.
3   ARRIVED MANILA.
3   DEPARTED.
3   ARRIVED SUBIC.
8   DEPARTED.
11 ARRIVED MINDORO.
11 DEPARTED.
12 ARRIVED SUBIC.
14 DEPARTED.
17 ARRIVED PARANG, MINDA
    NAO, P.I. AND BOMBARDED.
19 DEPARTED AREA.
21 ARRIVED SUBIC.
29 DEPARTED SUBIC.

DOWN FROM KYUSHU AND THE NANSEI SHOTO ISLANDS, AND LORD KNOWS WHERE ELSE, THE "DRAGONS," THE KIKUSAI (FLOATING CHRYS-ANTHEMUMS) PILOTS CAME. THESE SUICIDE PILOTS DID NOT ATTACK IN THE USUAL KAMIKAZE STRIKES OF TWO OR THREE...OR TEN, BUT IN MASSED FLIGHTS. THEY SCREAMED IN BY THE HUNDREDS, DAY BY DAY, WEEK AFTER WEEK. FOR MONTHS OKINAWA WOULD BE AN INFERNO.

MEANWHILE, THE STEVENS WAS OPER-ATING OFF MINDANAO, WHERE THE FIGHT FOR THE PHILIPPINES WAS STILL RAGING. AS MENTIONED, WE'D BEEN IN THE PACIFIC FOR 14 MONTHS. YET, IN ALL THAT TIME, WE HAD NOT BEEN WITHOUT "ENTERTAINMENT."

BRATTA TAT BOMBA BOOM RATTA TATTA TAT

A CREW MEMBER, BILL "GENE KRUPA" DOHENEY PLAYED ON HIS DRUMS...

NOT AGAIN!?

KNOCK IT OFF!

SOMEBODY KILL THAT #7%@!!

BY NOW, HE WAS DRIVING US ALL CRAZY.

DOHENEY'S DRUM AND THE HEAT BELOW DECKS WERE TOO MUCH FOR ME. DETERMINED MORE THAN EVER TO SLEEP TOPSIDE, ONCE AGAIN, WITH HAMMOCK IN HAND, I CLIMBED THE FORWARD STACK.

I HAD NOTICED THE SHIP WAS ALWAYS CONNED * TO MAKE A SWEEPING TURN TO STARBOARD WHENEVER TUBES WERE BLOWN. THIS KEPT MOST OF THE SOOT OFF THE SHIP, PARTICULARLY THE PORT SIDE.

*CONNED : STEERED.

DD 479

U.S.S. STEVENS
(TRAVEL LOG)

MAY
1   ARRIVED POLLOC HARBOR, MINDANAO.
2   DEPARTED.
3   ARRIVED DAVAO GULF.
4   DEPARTED.
8-12   EXERCISES.
17   ARRIVED MANILA.
21   DEPARTED.
21   ARRIVED SUBIC.
23   DEPARTED.
23   ARRIVED MANILA.
28   DEPARTED.
28-31   EXERCISES.

WELL, I GOT MY HAMMOCK SLUNG BETWEEN THE SEARCHLIGHT AND THE GUARDRAIL ON THE PORT SIDE. I'M CUDDLED UP PRETTY COMFY, JUST STARTIN' TO DOZE OFF, WHEN I HEARD THIS CLATTER OF FEET COMIN' UP THE LADDER... A COUPL'A CURSES, #$!@?!# ...SOMEBODY WAS TRYIN' TO UNDO THE HITCHES ON MY HAMMOCK. A COUPL'A MORE CURSES, *?$%@ AND SOMEBODY GROWLED, "CUT THE #!?#@# LINE!"

BONK! DOWN I GO.

WHAT THE HECK YOU GUYS DOIN'?

SHUT UP!

I COULD SEE THE TALKER. (THE GUY WITH THE HEADSET). HE WAS IN-STRUCTIN' THE GUY FIDDLIN' WITH THE SEARCHLIGHT.

JOE! SWING 'ER TO 260°!! WHEN I GIVE YOU THE WORD, FLICK 'ER ON!

SAM! GETCHA #$!?@ HAMMOCK OUTTA HERE! RADAR JUST PICKED UP SOMETHING OUT IN THE WATER!

MAYBE I WAS DREAMIN', BUT I SWEAR, IT SEEMED LIKE OUR ENGINES WERE CUT DOWN AND GQ WASN'T EVEN SOUNDED. IT DIDN'T FIGURE. IT WAS LIKE WE WERE TRYIN' TO "SNEAK" UP ON SOMETHING. IT WAS REALLY WEIRD.

I COULDN'T SEE A DARN THING. BUT I KNEW THE GUNNERS WERE ALL AT THEIR STATIONS. I HEARD THE 5"/38s WHIRL AROUND, THE 40s CLANKIN', AN' THE 20s... AND EVEN THE TORPEDO TUBES. YEAH! FELT THE SHIP HEAVE A SIGH WHEN THEY WERE TRAINED OUTBOARD.

SOMETHING WAS OUT THERE, ALL RIGHT. AND, IN A SECOND, THE SEARCHLIGHTS WOULD BE FLICKED ON.

WHOOMP!! TOTAL DARKNESS BECAME BRILLIANT DAYLIGHT. CAUGHT IN THE SUDDEN GLARE WAS A CHINESE FISHING BOAT.

110

ON THE BOAT'S STERN, SQUATTING OVER, THINKING HE WAS ALL ALONE IN THAT VAST OCEAN, PROBABLY LOOKIN' AT THE STARS AN' MEDITATIN' WITH THE 'UNIVERSE WAS A CHINAMAN... RELIEVING HIS BOWELS.

WHEN THAT LIGHT HIT, IT SCARED THE STUFFIN'S OUTTA HIM. THAT FELLER MUST'A POPPED SIX FEET IN THE AIR. ARMS A' FLAPPIN', FEET A' PUMPIN', AND MOUTH A' SCREAMIN'!

TURNED OUT HE WAS A FRIENDLY. QUITE A FEW OF THESE FISHING BOATS PICKED UP MANY A DOWNED AMERICAN FLIER.

AT BALIKPAPEN, AS PART OF A BOMBARDMENT GROUP, WE SUPPORTED SOME MINESWEEPERS AND BOMBARDED THE BEACHES AT KLANDASAN.

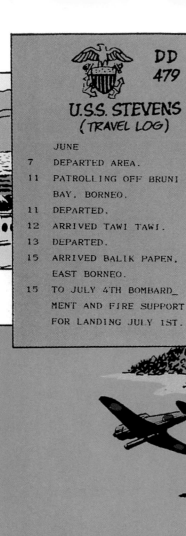

DD 479

U.S.S. STEVENS
(TRAVEL LOG)

JUNE
7   DEPARTED AREA.
11   PATROLLING OFF BRUNI BAY, BORNEO.
11   DEPARTED.
12   ARRIVED TAWI TAWI.
13   DEPARTED.
15   ARRIVED BALIK PAPEN, EAST BORNEO.
15   TO JULY 4TH BOMBARD_MENT AND FIRE SUPPORT FOR LANDING JULY 1ST.

DURING NIGHT RETIREMENT (JUST BEFORE DUSK WE'D MOVE OUT TO SEA TO GAIN SEA ROOM *), OUR GROUP CAME UNDER AIR ATTACK. I MENTION THIS PARTICULAR ATTACK BECAUSE WE WERE REALLY CAUGHT OFF GUARD.

THE PLANES CAME IN LOW OVER THE WATER. BECAUSE OF THE LARGE LAND MASS, RADAR DIDN'T PICK 'EM UP. BUT, FORTUNATELY, OUR GUNNERS WERE ALREADY AT THEIR GQ STATIONS (DUSK ALERTS HAD BECOME A DAILY ROUTINE). SO, ALTHOUGH RADAR FAILED TO PICK THE PLANES UP, OUR GROUP PICKED 'EM OFF.

THE NEXT DAY "GENE KRUPA" HELD A RAFFLE FOR A BUCK A CHANCE. THE WINNER GOT THE PRIVILEGE TO KICK IN HIS DRUM AND "DEEP SIX" IT.

*SEA ROOM: FAR ENOUGH AWAY FROM LAND FOR UNRESTRICTED MOVEMENT OF SHIPS.

HE PROBABLY THOUGHT SOMEONE WOULD EVENTUALLY DO IT ANYWAY.

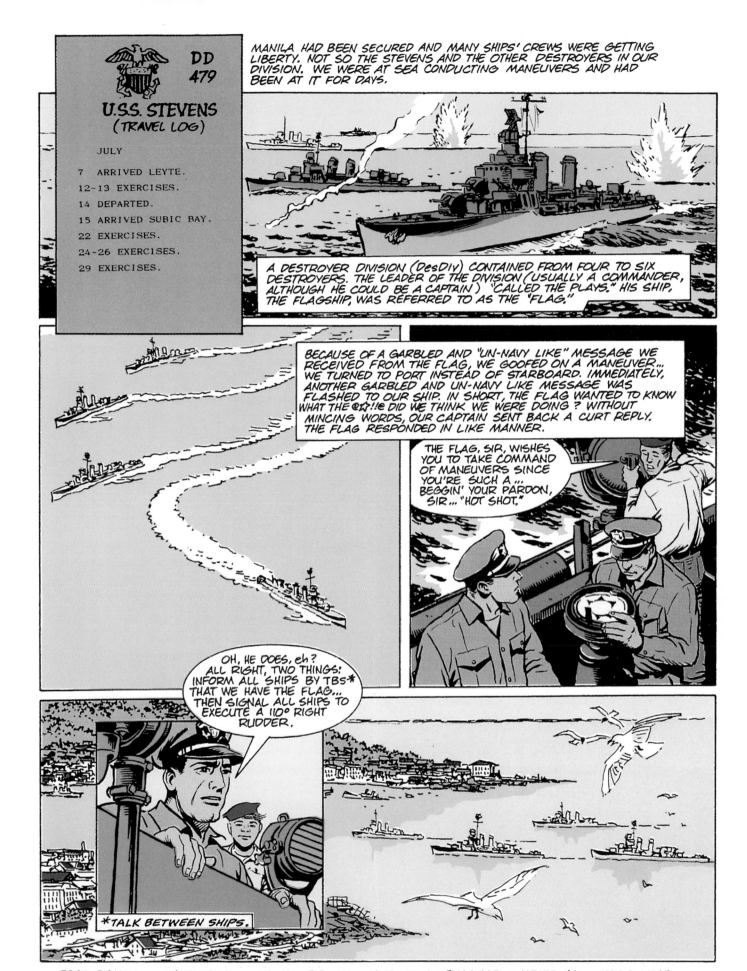

MANILA HAD BEEN SECURED AND MANY SHIPS' CREWS WERE GETTING LIBERTY. NOT SO THE STEVENS AND THE OTHER DESTROYERS IN OUR DIVISION. WE WERE AT SEA CONDUCTING MANEUVERS AND HAD BEEN AT IT FOR DAYS.

DD 479

U.S.S. STEVENS
(TRAVEL LOG)

JULY

7   ARRIVED LEYTE.
12-13 EXERCISES.
14   DEPARTED.
15   ARRIVED SUBIC BAY.
22   EXERCISES.
24-26 EXERCISES.
29   EXERCISES.

A DESTROYER DIVISION (DesDiv) CONTAINED FROM FOUR TO SIX DESTROYERS. THE LEADER OF THE DIVISION (USUALLY A COMMANDER, ALTHOUGH HE COULD BE A CAPTAIN) "CALLED THE PLAYS." HIS SHIP, THE FLAGSHIP, WAS REFERRED TO AS THE "FLAG."

BECAUSE OF A GARBLED AND "UN-NAVY LIKE" MESSAGE WE RECEIVED FROM THE FLAG, WE GOOFED ON A MANEUVER... WE TURNED TO PORT INSTEAD OF STARBOARD. IMMEDIATELY, ANOTHER GARBLED AND UN-NAVY LIKE MESSAGE WAS FLASHED TO OUR SHIP. IN SHORT, THE FLAG WANTED TO KNOW WHAT THE @☆!!@ DID WE THINK WE WERE DOING? WITHOUT MINCING WORDS, OUR CAPTAIN SENT BACK A CURT REPLY. THE FLAG RESPONDED IN LIKE MANNER.

THE FLAG, SIR, WISHES YOU TO TAKE COMMAND OF MANEUVERS SINCE YOU'RE SUCH A... BEGGIN' YOUR PARDON, SIR... "HOT SHOT."

OH, HE DOES, eh? ALL RIGHT, TWO THINGS: INFORM ALL SHIPS BY TBS* THAT WE HAVE THE FLAG,... THEN SIGNAL ALL SHIPS TO EXECUTE A 110° RIGHT RUDDER.

*TALK BETWEEN SHIPS.

DEAR READER -- MY NOMENCLATURE MAY BE INCORRECT. AS AN ENGINEER, I NEVER HAD DUTY ON THE BRIDGE. NEVERTHELESS, OUR SKIPPER "MANEUVERED" THE SQUADRON RIGHT INTO MANILA HARBOR AND ALL HANDS WERE GRANTED LIBERTY.

THIS WAS THE FIRST LIBERTY WE'D HAD IN A TOWN FOR LORD KNOWS HOW LONG. BUT IT WAS MORE LIKE WALKING AROUND IN AN ABANDONED BRICK PILE. MANILA HAD BEEN HIT BAD.

...AND APPARENTLY THEY HADN'T QUITE CLEANED UP.

THESE INNOCENT PEOPLE HAD BEEN BOMBED AND SHOT AND BEATEN WHEN THE JAPANESE FIRST INVADED THE PHILIPPINES IN 1941. IN 1944, THE INNOCENT SUFFERED AGAIN... CAUGHT IN THE MIDDLE WHEN U.S. AND JAPANESE FORCES CLASHED IN THE BATTLE FOR MANILA. 100,000 FILIPINO CIVILIANS DIED, NEARLY SIX TIMES THE AMOUNT OF SOLDIERS KILLED ON BOTH SIDES.

THE PEOPLE WERE LIVING ON THE OUTSKIRTS, IN A FEW BUILDINGS STILL STANDING, IN SHACKS AND LEAN-TOS. THEY WERE ALL WELL SPOKEN AND EDUCATED. LAWYERS, CLERKS, MERCHANTS, YOUR "NEXT DOOR" TYPE OF NEIGHBOR.

A GREAT NUMBER WERE CRIPPLED, SICK, HUNGRY, AND HELPLESS. THEIR LIVES WERE SHATTERED, THEIR POSSESSIONS DESTROYED.

IT SEEMED EVERYONE WAS "SOLICITING"--THEMSELVES, WIVES, DAUGHTERS, AND SISTERS-- IN ORDER TO SURVIVE. IT WAS GOD-AWFUL DISTRESSING...

...I GOT DRUNK.

AGAIN I GOT LIBERTY. THIS TIME I STAYED IN TOWN... WHAT WAS LEFT OF MANILA.

I WALKED PAST SANTA CRUZ CHURCH, PAST THE FINANCE BUILDING, AND PAST THE ONCE-FINE METROPOLITAN THEATER.

I WAS ASTONISHED BY THE SIZE AND GRANDEUR OF THE MANILA POST OFFICE.

IN SOLEMN SILENCE, I STOOD IN FRONT OF THE RUINS OF VILLAMOR HALL AT THE UNIVERSITY OF THE PHILIPPINES.

THE CHILDREN THAT HAD ATTENDED IT... WHAT WOULD BECOME OF THEIR DREAMS?

LATER I CAME ACROSS MY BUDDY, PINKY. THE TWO OF US RETURNED TO OUR SHIP.

NEXT DAY ABOARD SHIP, I FOUND BO'S'N E. SMITH BUSY SEWING.

WHAT'S THAT?

GOING HOME PENNANT.*

PENNANT?

YEAH. YOU HEARD WE BEAT THE NAZIS, RIGHT?

YEAH. SO?

OUR SHIPS ARE OFFSHORE SHELLING HONSHU AND OUR PLANES ARE BOMBING TOKYO, RIGHT?

SO??

SO, I'M MAKING OUR GOING HOME PENNANT. WE'LL BE GOING HOME SOON.'

I WASN'T CONVINCED. THERE'D BEEN SCUTTLEBUTT ABOUT THE JAPANESE MAKING A LAST DITCH SUICIDE STAND ON JAPAN.

*GOING HOME PENNANT: AN OLD NAVY TRADITION. WHEN WE WENT HOME, WE FLEW THIS MULTI-COLORED FLAG. IT REACHED FROM THE FORWARD MAST ALL THE WAY TO THE STERN. IT HAD TO BE HELD UP ON THE END WITH A WEATHER BALLOON.

"BOATS" WAS RIGHT. BUT IT WOULD BE ANOTHER FOUR MONTHS BEFORE WE HEADED FOR HOME.

MEANWHILE, I HAD ONE MORE LIBERTY IN THE PHILIPPINES. THIS TIME I HUNG AROUND THE BEACH HOPING TO GET SOME SOUVENIRS FROM THE ARMY GUYS.

WE NAVY GUYS HADN'T HAD MUCH CHANCE TO GET SOUVENIRS. THE ONLY THING I HAVE IS A PIECE OF METAL I'VE BEEN WEARING FOR THE PAST 44 YEARS.

ANYWAY, I WANDERED INTO A HUGE ARMY TENT. INSIDE, A CRAP GAME WAS UNDERWAY.

THE GUY RUNNING IT HAD A BIG BOX FULL OF MONEY IN FRONT OF HIM AND TWO BIG "GUARDS" BEHIND HIM.

DURING THE GAME, I MADE A SIDE BET WITH SOME JOKER AN' WON THE MOST BEAUTIFUL PAIR OF TAILOR-MADE "BLUES"* YOU EVER SAW. BACK ABOARD SHIP ...

...I TRIED 'EM ON, PERFECT FIT, EVEN HAD MY RATE ON 'EM. UNDRESS WHITES WITH KERCHIEF IS WHAT WE WORE FOR LIBERTY OUT HERE (THE NAVY HAD GOTTEN RID OF DRESS WHITES A LONG TIME AGO). ANYWAY, THESE DRESS BLUES I STOWED AWAY FOR STATESIDE LIBERTY WHERE I COULD WEAR 'EM.

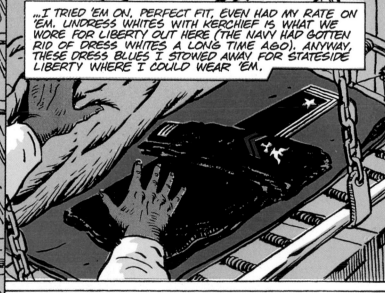

*"BLUES": DRESS UNIFORM

ABOARD SHIP, IF WE WANTED TO PRESS OUR CLOTHES, WE'D PUT THEM UNDER OUR MATTRESS.

DD
479

U.S.S. STEVENS
(TRAVEL LOG)

AUGUST
2 DEPARTED SUBIC BAY
6 ARRIVED MANILA
14 EXERCISES
15 16 17 EXERCISES
19 UNDERWAY FOR MANILA
19 DEPARTED MANILA
19 ARRIVED SUBIC
28 DEPARTED SUBIC
30 ARRIVED OKINAWA

Off Kume Shima, Keisan Sho and Kerama Retto, the "Lost Harbor," one could actually feel the presence of the souls of those brave American seamen that lost their lives here at Okinawa. —And, one could also feel the presence of the misguided, perhaps, but nevertheless equally brave, Kikusui pilots that screamed in like dragons.

For the destroyer men at Okinawa, the horror began on April 6th, 1945. The sea and the sky burst into flame. Destroyer gunners on picket duty, fighting for their lives, blew away plane after plane. . .yet, like streaking shadows, more and more Kamikaze came to smash against the ships.

Most exploded when they hit.

Destroyers Haynesworth, Hyman, Howorth, Morris, Leutze, Hutchins, Harrison, Mullany, Newcomb, and destroyer-escort Fieberling were hit. Mutilated and disabled, destroyers began to crawl to sanctuaries at Guam, the Philippines, and Kerama Retto.

...lost April 6th: U.S.S. Bush with 87 men dead.

8-inch thunderbolts and steady firehose streams of white-hot tracers were pumped into the attacking planes. For two days they had swarmed over the ship. On the third day, just 30 feet above the water, a Kamikaze rushed in with the speed of a locomotive. It smashed into the ship's starboard side between stacks no. 1 and 2. The explosion hurled a 4,000 pound section of the engine room's blower 50 feet into the air. A second suicider hit, nearly cutting the ship in half. Topside bluejackets died in the inferno; below decks, others died drowning in the inrushing waters. In agony the ship struggled to remain afloat. A third plane plummeted in, erupting with a crimson flash... ending the agony. Wallowing in flood water and flame, the ship broke apart and sank.

April 6th...   U.S.S. Calhoun lost with 35 men dead.
Scores of crippled vessels went limping to sanctuary. By April 11th, destroyers Hale, Hank, Kidd, Charles J. Badger, Gregory, Bennett, Hutchins and destroyer-escorts Wesson and Manlove would be hit.

April 12th, President Roosevelt died. To celebrate, the Kamikaze "Dragons" came in a monster assault, over 200 strong. Destroyer Stanley, Bennion, Purdy, and Cassin Young were hit. Destroyer-escorts Whitehurst, Riddle, and Rall were hit. The battleships Tennessee and Idaho were hit. . .and on destroyer Mannert L. Abele, men and machinery were blasted sky-high by an exploding suicider. Seconds later, the forward fireroom erupted, hit by a baka bomb. In three minutes the ship sank, taking with her the dead, charred, and mangled bodies of 73 men. Four days later, working with destroyer-minelayer Hobson, the U.S.S. Pringle was sunk. 62 men died. April 16th, destroyer McDermut was hit, as were Laffey and Bryant and destroyer-escort Bowers. Kerama Retto became crowded with cripples.

Every day at Okinawa was a 24-hour ordeal. "Pips" appeared on radar screens like snowflakes. Death approached the ships in a growing roar as Japanese planes streaked in. U.S.S. Little sunk May 3rd. U.S.S. Luce sunk May 4th. U.S.S. Morrison was on radar picket station no. 1 as fighter-director: her ordeal occurred shortly after Luce was sunk. The carnage began when in a mass murder-and-suicide assault——within two-minute intervals, four suiciders struck. At least two carried bombs. With her vitals torn out, mutilated, spewing smoke and flame, Morrison went under. She sank so quickly that there was not time to abandon ship. Most men below decks were lost. Out of 331 men, 152 died.

In an attempt to stem this awful tide of Kamikaze flights, all available American aircraft made bombing attacks on suspected Japanese air-fields. But the kamikaze lairs were hard to find. Brooding in secret nests, the "Dragons" kept coming.

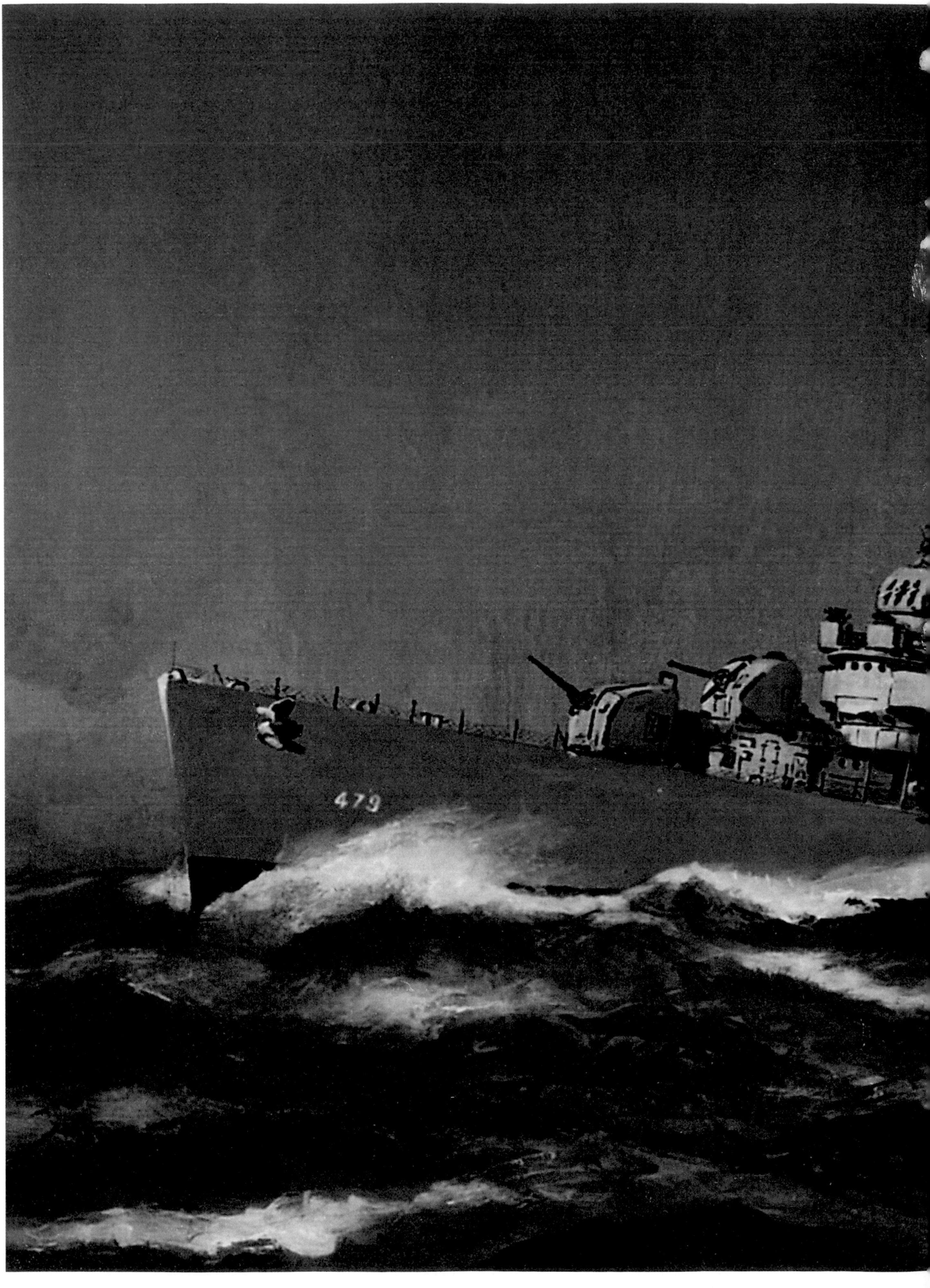
479

TRIBUTES

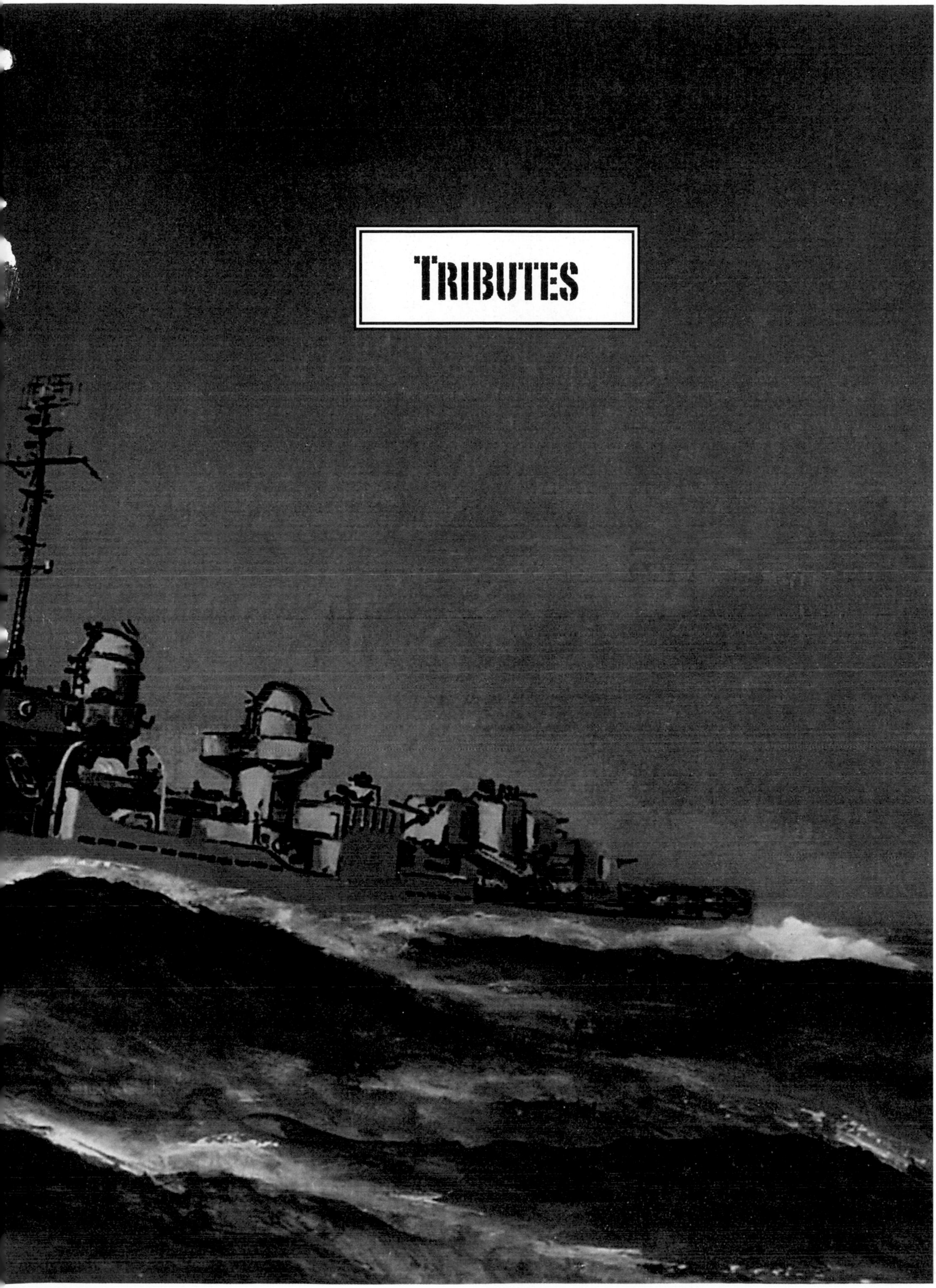

GEORGE PRATT

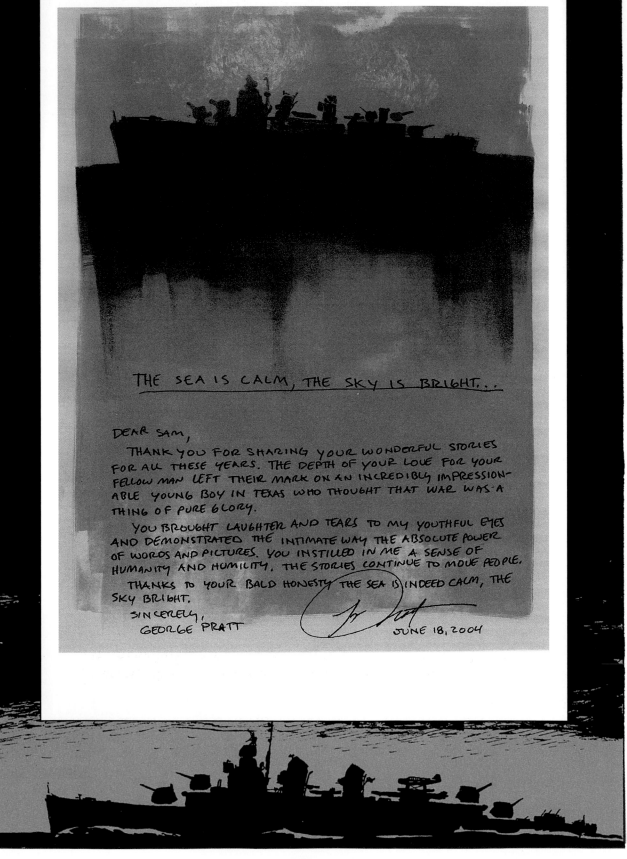

THE SEA IS CALM, THE SKY IS BRIGHT...

DEAR SAM,
   THANK YOU FOR SHARING YOUR WONDERFUL STORIES
FOR ALL THESE YEARS. THE DEPTH OF YOUR LOVE FOR YOUR
FELLOW MAN LEFT THEIR MARK ON AN INCREDIBLY IMPRESSION-
ABLE YOUNG BOY IN TEXAS WHO THOUGHT THAT WAR WAS A
THING OF PURE GLORY.
   YOU BROUGHT LAUGHTER AND TEARS TO MY YOUTHFUL EYES
AND DEMONSTRATED THE INTIMATE WAY THE ABSOLUTE POWER
OF WORDS AND PICTURES. YOU INSTILLED IN ME A SENSE OF
HUMANITY AND HUMILITY. THE STORIES CONTINUE TO MOVE PEOPLE.
   THANKS TO YOUR BALD HONESTY THE SEA IS INDEED CALM, THE
SKY BRIGHT.
   SINCERELY,
   GEORGE PRATT
                                    JUNE 18, 2004

BEAU SMITH

"Sam Glanzman: When a Friend Is a Friend"

When I hear the term "Free Spirit," I think of Sam Glanzman. In my opinion, Sam has always been a perfect example of free-thinking, creativity, intelligence, and being a couple of steps ahead of everyone else without conceit or bragging.

Growing up, I knew that the artist Sam Glanzman could draw really cool dinosaurs, battleships, and tanks, and that was always more than enough for me. If Sam's name was on the comic book, then I knew it was a risk-free purchase for me. Even in grade school I could figure that math out.

Sam has always remained on my "go to" list. If he was connected to a project, then I knew I could buy it and be more than satisfied. I can't think of a time when Sam has let me down. When I began getting into comic books on the business and writing end, one of my first contacts was with DC Comics editor Murray Boltinoff. He was always very kind to me and treated me as a peer from the start—I always appreciated his respect, which I felt I hadn't quite earned yet. Murray gave me tips, introduced me to a couple of lifetime friends and mentors, Joe Kubert and Robert Kanigher, and told me that if I ever got the chance to meet or work with Sam Glanzman, I should jump on it. He said that not only was Sam as talented as Kubert, he was just as much a professional. Of course, being still awestruck by the mention of Sam's name, I put the chance of ever working with or knowing Sam up there with my other pie-in-the-sky dreams.

Soon after I officially began work as VP of marketing for Eclipse Comics, and as a writer, the opportunity to do some side marketing came up with my friends Tim Truman and Chuck Dixon on a project that they were working on called "4 Winds." They were going to publish and produce books and collections of projects that were near and dear to their own creative hearts. It was then that, along with a fellow artist and amigo, Gary Kwapisz, we found that we all held Sam Glanzman in high esteem. Being the same age, we all grew up enjoying Sam's art, and through Tim we all got to know Sam. We were going to publish his incredible sci-fi/adventure story *Attu*.

The thing that most people in comics never realized is that Sam is a heck of a writer, on top of being a great artist. His Marvel Comics graphic novel *A Sailor's Story* is still one my favorite books in the last 40 years. If ever anything needed to be made into a film, this was it.

Getting to become a friend of Sam's has been my biggest pleasure. He's a funny, witty, modest guy who knows a lot about everything—he can talk about any topic and still be modest about his knowledge of it. He's always been a physical guy, one who you'd never think could sit still long enough to draw. Today at 90, I'd guess that it would be hard for guys half his age to keep up with him mentally or physically. Sam would no doubt give you a "sucks and shuffle" about it, but trust me, never count him out.

I could always see Sam's influence in Tim Truman's work, even before Tim and I became good friends. I used to ponder if Sam was an influence when I would look at his comics. It's easy to see why these two guys are such good buddies.

I must say that the few times Sam has been down here to my house to visit were great. Sam drove his big RV, camped out here, and entertained my wife, Beth, and me with his tales and his humor. Sam was also a big hit with the waitresses who served us when we went out to eat. They all found him quite charming. One remarked that Sam reminded her of a shorter Sam Elliott (the actor), but I always thought Sam was a spitting image of the other actor/stuntman, Richard Farnsworth, even their voices were alike. I guess what I'm trying to say is that Sam always leaves an unforgettable impression.

He came through my office and not only recognized my Charles M. Russell prints, he whipped out the names of the prints instantly. We talked about Russell's work as well as that of Frederic Remington. I enjoyed going through my original art collection with Sam; he pointed out so many things about the pieces and I learned so much. Sam also could've been a great teacher or art director. Maybe he will be when he feels he has time. Nothing Sam does surprises me. He's an amazing guy.

A few weeks after Sam had been here, I got a package from him in the mail. It was a drawing he had done of me in one of the Remington drawings, "An Old Time Mountain Man With His Ponies." It's beautiful and one of my most treasured pieces, a part of Sam that will always be with me. I smile thinking of Sam and his dry sense of humor every time I look up at it.

I thank God for friends like Sam. He is truly a gift. Even today, I still find it mind-boggling that I am friends with THE Sam Glanzman who made my childhood and my life a little more exciting with his storytelling, both in print and in real life.

You are a very good friend, Sam, the best.

Your amigo,
Beau Smith
The Flying Fist Ranch

www.flyingfistranch.com

S.J.G. 1989   BEAU SMITH a la ———— REMINGTON

Stephen R. Bissette

I've been a devotee of Sam Glanzman's comics from a tender age—his war, adventure, and fantasy comics and stories for Gilberton (the *Classics Illustrated World Around Us* series), for Dell (*Combat, Voyage to the Deep, Kona, Flying Saucers,* etc.), for Charlton (*Attack, Battlefield Action, Fightin' Army, Tarzan of the Apes, Hercules,* etc.), for DC Comics (*Our Army at War, G.I. Combat,* etc.)—all of it. Even when I was a lad, I responded to an authenticity in Sam's artwork on a gut level: Sam's comics looked "lived in." His animals looked more alive, his jungles more steamy, his battle scenes more real than anything else in comics.

Sam's naturalistic approach to action was unusually frank: it looked as if he'd lived it. In many cases, it turns out he had. This naturalism informed even his most outré fantasy comics, but was most apparent in Glanzman's harrowing *Combat* stories for Dell, the first war comics of their generation to show us what war looked like. Having actively served in the U.S. Navy's Pacific theater during World War II, Sam showed us what the moon looked like seen from the deck of a submarine cutting through the ocean by night; what white-hot gunfire looked like when it was fired *right at you*; what it felt like when flesh-and-blood men were wounded; what happened when planes plunged into the ocean with pilots trapped in the cockpits; how sailors burned below molten decks as kamikaze fighters slammed into battleships. There was nothing sensationalistic or exploitative about Sam's depictions of such warfare: they just happened, they were *there*, clear on the page. For what it's worth, I can honestly say I have a career in comics because of Sam and his artwork: his was the first comics art I ever obsessed over, studied, and copied as meticulously and diligently as an inspired four-and-five-year old boy could.

With all due respect to Harvey Pekar (and I knew and loved Harvey), comics historians, fans, and academia seem to forget that before Pekar was "inventing" the memoir comic in the underground and alternative comics scenes, Glanzman had already been at it for years in mainstream newsstand comic books. As a reference point, remember that Glanzman's biographical *U.S.S. Stevens* stories in *Our Army At War* #218 (DC Comics, April 1970) set sail six years before Pekar debuted *American Splendor*. That through line—from Glanzman's illustrated letters home during WWII to the book you now hold in your hands—is ample evidence of how long overdue a celebration of Sam's unique and heroic stature in American comics history truly is. Here's to you, Sam!

CARL POTTS

As a kid in the mid-1960s, I bought a lot of WWII comics—mostly DC's line. DC's artists covered a range of styles but most were very polished: Joe Kubert, Russ Heath, Irv Novick, Ross Andru, and so on.

One day when I was scanning the comics' spinner rack at the local variety store, trying to figure out which DC war title to spend my hard-earned lawn-mowing coinage on, I spotted an issue of Dell's *Combat*. I picked it up and saw it was filled with great art by some guy named Sam Glanzman.

Instead of buying up the latest *Our Army at War* starring Sgt. Rock, *All American Men of War* featuring Johnny Cloud tale, or *Star Spangled War Stories* (dinosaurs in WWII!) from DC, I plunked down my 12 cents for that issue of *Combat* and devoured it. After that, I kept my eye open for any title that contained Sam Glanzman's distinctive and authentic work.

CHRIS CLAREMONT

It's getting on towards 75 years since the Japanese attack on Pearl Harbor cast the United States headlong onto the battlefields of World War II. This passage of time has transformed these events from the immediacy of recent history to the tales told by parents and grandparents. Their presentation in popular media has ranged from radio plays and films and television show to novels and historical treatises almost beyond number, relating the stories and events from the most globally significant to the most supremely personal. Sam Glanzman's *A Sailor's Story* uses the medium of comics to accomplish both goals. This is a rare and valued accomplishment. My own father-in-law had honorable service aboard another destroyer, the USS *Evans*, until the ship was knocked out of action at Okinawa by three Japanese kamikaze hits, but like many veterans he rarely talked about what happened. With *A Sailor's Story*, Sam uses his skills as both graphic artist and writer to bring those long-past events to visual life—to viscerally transport the readers back to those dramatic days when the United States was fighting on two oceans and three continents to safeguard the future of the world. This isn't a story of make-believe super-beings; these are real people, with real fears, being transformed by events and circumstances into men of courage, doing what had to be done in this global conflict. Some were heroes; all have earned the right to be remembered. Sam's album does that most eloquently and is something we *all* should read.

Denny O'Neil

I was lucky enough to know Sam when I was the new kid on the block and he was a respected veteran. He was, first, a gentleman— nicer to me than he had any need to be.

And he seemed deeply invested in his stories about life in the Navy. They were probably autobiographical and so more than just jobs. He put himself into the work and I salute him for what he accomplished.

Kurt Busiek

Sam Glanzman has to be one of the most honest, dedicated and engaging cartoonists in the history of comics. His artwork has always been engaging, and his stories—especially the autobiographical tales of his times on the *U.S.S. Stevens*—are endlessly fascinating, as we've been privileged to see him build a nuanced, powerful living document that brings the WWII experience alive in a way that no history book can compete with. His work isn't just terrifically entertaining; it's a unique and valuable treasure, both to comics and to history.

Stan Lee

Sam Glanzman is one of the most neglected stars. It's a shame that a talent like his has been so overlooked when writing about those who made comic books the exciting medium they are.

Paul Levitz

In a long and solid career in comics, Sam may have peaked by becoming the first cartoonist to take the genre formula of war comics and turn it on its head with his personal memoirs in the *U.S.S. Stevens* stories. A bit of quiet pioneering that's been underappreciated.

JOE R. LANSDALE

I had the honor to work with Sam Glanzman on several projects, in conjunction with Tim Truman, another fine artist. But the project I enjoyed working on with Sam the most was *Red Range*. This was a project I wrote and he illustrated. It was just me and him. It was an odd ball, weird-ass, black-and-white Western that I wrote for a now defunct book company, MOJO PRESS, that ventured into comics briefly.

Red Range was written as if it was the first in a saga of stories about the character Red Range, a black cowboy who disguises himself in a kind of Lone Ranger–style way and fights crime and prejudice against blacks in the Old West. It came complete with a crazed villain, shoot-outs, and roughhousing, and finally a venture to a lost valley that led to the center of the Earth. There were dinosaurs and a variety of weird races, and it was my plan that if it caught on, I would do a volume two and a volume three.

It didn't catch on, but working with Sam made it worth it. He was professional, fast, and just amazing. He could draw people and flora and fauna, and had a nifty touch when it came to dinosaurs. He was on time and just honorable all the way. It was cool to see the black-and-white images he drew, and his pages excited me to no end. I had already begun to collect work by him, though considering how much he has done, my collection is sadly minimal, so I was well aware of his importance in the history of comics, an importance that is underrated, partly due to Sam's own impressive modesty. If I had his talent I'd climb a flag pole and yell out, "Hey, look at this stuff. I'm great." But not Sam. He just took his brilliance in stride.

Ultimately, the only thing that matters here is that Sam is not only one swell guy, he is one of the finest artists working today, and I don't even think he knows it (and if he does, his aforementioned modesty doesn't allow him to let us know he knows)—wonderful lines and images, and even suggestive lines that tell more of a story than more complicated drawings by some better-known artist. Talk about a master, you have to talk about Sam Glanzman.

My hope is that younger artists will become aware of his work, and learn something from him, because certainly they could.

JOE KUBERT

Monday, Dec 14, '87

Dear Sam—

I've been waitin' for a little bit of time to sit and read "A Sailor's Story"—and yesterday 'n today were the days—and the time.

I can't begin to tell you how THOROUGHLY I enjoyed the book. I remember some of the sketches 'n basic stories you showed me—or that we published—when you were doing the "STEVENS" stuff. But lacing it all together as you've done—was GREAT! Some of the scenes—like PG. 16—the planes coming in at dusk—everything muted in color, except for the flashes from the planes' engines, and a little white on the white caps breaking around the ship—JUST RIGHT!

There were other outstanding panels in color—but, what did it for ME was the STORY—and the story telling.

Every scene—every sequence—every reference point was absolutely credible 'n believable. Of course they were—because it was all TRUE!

Now, one might say, "of course it's believable! It WAS TRUE!" But, it doesn't necessarily follow that true stories can be told so that truth can be RECOGNIZED.

THAT, SAM, you DID!

That's because you put a little piece of YOURSELF in 'n on every GODDAM page.

It's a book to be PROUD of, Sam—'n I'M proud of you, too. It's really a FINE, FINE JOB!

Take care—'n keep it sailin'!

Yours,

Joe

P.S. I've been told you're starting on book #2. TERRIFIC!

SAM—
THOSE DEADLINES'LL
GETCHA *EVERY TIME!*
WITH AFFECTION — JOE KUBERT

STEVE FEARS

Sam Glanzman Is My Friend

When I was young, I discovered comic books and grew to enjoy reading them—especially the war comics. I read a lot of DC war comics, Charlton, and Dell. While reading the Charlton and Dell comics, I became a fan of a certain artist who signed his work "Sam Glanzman." There were other artists that I liked, such as Joe Kubert, Russ Heath, and Jerry Grandenetti, but Sam Glanzman was high on my list.

I found the Dell comics—**War Stories Combat**, **Air War Stories**, **World War Stories** —among my favorites. Many of the Charlton war comics with Sam's art were also some of the comic books I liked to read.

Sam then joined the artists at DC Comics and began illustrating *The Haunted Tank* in **G.I. Combat**. I loved those! However, his series the *U.S.S. Stevens* became one of my favorites. These are some of the most important comic stories ever written, illustrated, or published! Sam put his heart and soul into those stories. They weren't some Hollywood idealized version of World War II stories; they were the real deal! They were personal because they were from his personal experiences in WWII. This series is his masterpiece and should be read by all war comic book fans.

Jumping ahead into the late 1990s, I had the honor of becoming a member of a group called the Big Five Collectors. These were a bunch of guys who collected mainly DC war comics, and they also try to get together during Comic-Con International. Some of those war comics' creators have been guests at some of their dinners. I went to a few of those and have met Russ Heath, Joe Kubert, Mort Drucker, Ric Estrada, John Severin, and others—and one of these others was Sam Glanzman! Meeting him was a dream come true!

Over the years, I've gotten to know Sam much better for the wonderful person that he is. He is kind, generous, and has a heart as big as the universe. You won't meet a better person anywhere. He is one-of-a-kind! My life has been enriched because of Sam Glanzman. Being a friend of Sam means a lot to me.

Who knew that when I started reading those comic books I would one day meet the man himself! You never know where your path will lead in life, but the journey is one of good fortune because I got to meet Sam. My life has truly been blessed!

Thank you, Sam, for the great stories and art that you have given me and so many, many others! And, above all, thank you for your friendship! I am very, very lucky!

Thomas Yeates

Sam Glanzman, or SJG, was just about the first comic artist name I was ever aware of. Sometime in the mid-sixties, I picked up a war comic, probably titled COMBAT, probably because I liked the COMBAT TV show. The comic book was not connected to the TV show, but I liked it anyway. There was a short story where a Japanese plane lands in Hawaii after bombing Pearl Harbor, an American soldier sees it, there's a fight, and the American wins. Just a little story told pretty much without text, but with heart instead. Sam's storytelling, straightforward drawing style, and subject matter all worked extremely well for me. It wasn't perfect, but it had energy, honesty, and FEELING. Since then I've always been aware of his instantly recognizable style and have picked up various projects of his through the years. Sam's short run of Tarzan comics for Charlton was absolutely terrific. When I attended the Joe Kubert School in the late seventies, Sam was one of the artists who were held in high esteem, particularly by Kubert, Steve Bissette, and myself. I fondly remember looking through DC war comics for Sam's amazing "Battle Album" installments. Some years back I met Sam at a San Diego convention and enjoyed the man as much as his art. He was looking for work, so a year or so later I hired him to do some layouts for me. He worked on *ODYSSEUS Escaping Poseidon's Curse*, and *ARTHUR and LANCELOT: The Fight for Camelot*. Both are young readers' graphic novels for Lerner Publishing. Working with Sam was a joy, and the books were improved by his excellent contributions. He is a fantastic guy and a fantastic artist.

Here's to ya, Sam!

TIMOTHY TRUMAN

My Buddy Sam

Thank God for cousins.

During my grade school years in the '60s, Dad would often load the family into our Dodge and together we'd drive across a couple of counties for a weekend visit with his brothers and sisters. I loved these trips. I got along great with my older cousins. There always seemed to be some sort of dangerous mischief to get into (I have a broken nose to verify that).

And besides, they had tons of comic books.

Unlike a lot of neophyte comic book readers, I tended to follow art styles rather than characters, titles, or publishing houses. The artists drawing the books were my superheroes. It is through my cousins' collections that I first experienced the work of guys who would become my earliest artistic heroes: Jack Kirby, Dick Ayers, Joe Kubert, Steve Ditko, Will Eisner, and a fellow named Sam Glanzman.

Sam's style reminded me of Joe Kubert's in many ways (Sam loves Joe's work and took it as a compliment the first time that I admitted this to him). The similarities are mainly in their inking techniques—the brisk, loose brush and pen strokes that they favor. Both are master storytellers. Both have an incredible knack for conveying a believable and lush "sense of place" in the locations in which they place their characters. Joe and Sam both realize the importance of the accuracy of mechanical details. And both are masters of characterization, body language, and expression.

However, there are many ways that their work is obviously different. For one thing, their styles are immediately identifiable. Joe's work seems to have a film of bomb-blasted sandstone dust on it. Sam's work is warmer. Joe's characters often seem grim, brooding, and battle weary. Sam's characters are just as battle hardened, but seem like folks that one could hang out with—heroes who a kid could be protected by rather than intimidated by.

Joe's layouts are masterfully cinematic. Sam's work is also informed by film, but also by great illustrators whose work he and his brother, Louis Glanzman, grew up on.

The first works of Sam's that I encountered were his great COMBAT WAR STORIES comics. Most issues of this series are truly neglected masterpieces in the catalog of American war and historical comics. It is in COMBAT that Sam's work is seen at its most "illustrative." The issues often led off with splash pages that are as masterfully composed as any single illustration that has ever been produced. Various scenes and characterizations pack as much impact and raw, true, discernable emotion as can be found on any comic book page ever published. Unlike the characters in many comics of the period, the people in Sam's COMBAT comics do not merely recite lines and go through static, two-dimensional poses. His characters *act*. As I hinted at above, Sam's pages also have this amazing sense of location to them. A vet himself (and one who kept sketch books of the things he saw and who illustrated the letters that he sent back home to his family—more on these later), Sam *knew* the feelings and scenes of warfare that he was depicting. In any event, though he will often discount them when one asks him about them, Sam's COMBAT WAR STORIES (and the title's sister book AIR WAR STORIES) were perhaps the finest documentary comics of their era (even more real and believable than EC's TWO-FISTED TALES, in my opinion). When they were topped, it was Sam himself who topped them, with his *U.S.S. Stevens* backup stories for DC and two graphic novels for Marvel.

During the same era, Sam was producing another title that had equally as much impact on me—KONA: MONARCH OF MONSTER ISLE. The image of the platinum-haired, bayonet-wielding Kona was, for me, as much a role model for the way to depict heroes as the work of Frazetta and Steranko, to follow. And when I saw Sam's depiction of one of the series' villains, Tommy, wielding a submarine gun as he sat astride a triceratops, forget it. My path to doing my own brand of adventure comics was laid before me.

Imagine my joy when, years later, I got the chance to work with my hero, Sam, on several projects. One of Sam's biggest influences was Hal Foster. Well, for me, working with Sam has always been like Sam getting a chance to work with Hal Foster. Of course, Sam will characteristically blush and shuffle his feet and shy away when he reads this. But it's true, Sam. So shut up and get back over here.

Sam Glanzman is one of my greatest artistic heroes. He is also my friend. And for that fact I am eternally grateful and humbled.

Residing at my house right now, in safe keeping, are hundreds of drawings and illustrated letters that Sam did when he as serving in the Pacific in World War II. These were the scenes form his life upon which he would later base most of his *Stevens* stories. The drawings comprise an incredibly rich and invaluable first-hand eyewitness account of history. Someday they will be published. If it's the last thing I do, they will be published.

In any event, here's to Sailor Sam Glanzman: swabbie with a brush; illustrator, writer, woodworker, motorcycle jockey, husband, father, good guy. Just don't compliment him too much. He doesn't like that.

Which means that I'm in real hot water right now.

WILL FRANZ ON SAM J. GLANZMAN

"…Bring your swipe files, Willi…"

I have never been a "comics" fan. I grew up in the 1950s and early '60s enjoying CLASSICS ILLUSTRATED and several titles by Dell Publishing. Characters such as Batman and Superman never interested me.

I had long admired the detail, grit and emotional quality of the illustrations of *"SJG"* in the COMBAT series, so I wrote to the artist, Sam Glanzman, through Dell Publishing sometime in 1965. I had included several of my own drawings with my letter and asked Sam (he signed his full name rather than only his initials on COMBAT's Dunkirk issue) for some advice on getting into the writing/illustration field. He answered my letter with some very kind and encouraging remarks and constructive critiques about my drawings and said that he would like to meet with me at his home…. He also said that I should bring my "swipe files."

Swipe Files are important reference materials that illustrators collect and use for accuracy in their work. Sam had been impressed with the details of my military drawings and figured that I must have some terrific swipe files of my own.

I boarded the Long Island Railroad at Brooklyn's Flatbush Avenue and met Sam in Commack in Suffolk County, New York. After meeting his wife, Barbara, who made us lunch, Sam asked to see my swipe files. I opened my attaché case and showed Sam… every issue of COMBAT that I had. Oh, I also had a few paperbacks of World War II photo accounts, but the majority of my research was Sam's own art.

Sam's face fell. Then he gave that wry smile and chuckle of his and admitted the truth. Sam, the stinker, was looking to either copy or rip off my swipe files for his own use!

Rather than the end, it was the beginning of one of the most treasured relationships of my life. I would sit there in awe watching Sam wield an ink-laden #2 Winsor & Newton sable brush on Bristol board the way the rest of us use a ball-point pen to sign our names on a check. With a few words and pencil strokes he would explain the principles of page layout and design. I was fifteen years old, and I believe that Sam had turned forty. I had recently been hit with a serious and chronic health issue that restricted my formal schooling so I had some extra time on my hands. Sam took an interest in my writing and showed me how to prepare a script for submission to Dick Giordano, editor at CHARLTON COMICS. Dick rejected my first efforts but wanted to see more. With Sam's encouragement, I kept at it, and eventually

Dick liked what he saw with *The Sniper. The Lonely War of Willy Schultz* and *The Iron Corporal* soon followed.

While my friends and peers were bagging groceries and stocking shelves, I was being published! I owe that wonderful opportunity and experience to Dick Giordano for taking a chance with me, an inexperienced 15-year-old kid who had never left Brooklyn! But I would never have met Dick Giordano if it hadn't been for the support and sponsorship of Sam Glanzman. Talk about taking a chance…

Our professional relationship together was all too brief. Over the years, Sam has remained a good and generous friend and respectful mentor. Although we didn't always agree, Sam never spoke down to me or treated me as an inferior. Sam treated me as a partner. He always advised and contributed to my development of a sound and disciplined creative process rather than merely criticizing my mistakes. He would listen and laugh and comment. And I would listen and learn because Sam has always been a man to listen to and learn from.

He taught me more than he realizes, and I have carried over and applied many of these lessons to other aspects of my life. I still write and teach today and try to structure my stories the way Sam crafted his pages of art. Never one to boast or brag, Sam demonstrated the value of a solid work ethic: "Always meet your deadline, Willi, 'cause others are depending on you…." I have enjoyed a number of Sam's little-seen humorous cartoons. He is a man who enjoys a good laugh. I also got to know something of his very spiritual nature as well, his tolerance, his love of family, and profound sentiments for his ship from the war in the Pacific, the destroyer DD 479 USS STEVENS.

With his genuine modesty and good nature, he is not one to appreciate his own talent the way others do. Sam's images conveyed the brutality, horror, and sadness of war. Uncompromising and honest, his renderings were not flashy or stylized, and nothing he portrayed would ever encourage a young person to participate in one. With all its blood, bewilderment and cruelty, the fear, boredom, the humor and irony of it all, Sam never glorified war or glamorized violence.

While many illustrators reduced the enemy to grotesque caricatures suited to wartime propaganda leaflets, Sam's portrayal of the enemy "grunt" expressed compassion, empathy, and respect for the guy on the other side caught up in the human tragedy of war. It is realism rare indeed.

Sam's work is frequently understated but tends to provoke serious thought rather than mere visual gratification. *The Battle of the Sunda Straight* in COM-

BAT #7 will always be the definitive "*SJG*" for me. The swift warships themselves seemed to come alive, and I shuddered at the fate of the three men on the grating above their ship's engine room when Japanese torpedoes struck home. Then, of course, there were *The Raid on Regensburg, Monte Casino, New Guinea,* and *Breakout at St. Lo.* Later there would be the USS STEVENS story when the disgusted Asian boatman, surviving with his family on U.S. Navy garbage, comments on the callous American sailors aboard the destroyer: "Warriors…What do they know of war?" The list is endless.

The years have gone by. Yeah, so Sam's occasionally a little forgetful and becomes slightly cantankerous now and then. Sam has always been a man of few words, but his words have always been honest and on the mark. He is a man who cares.

Sam Glanzman is a man of warmth, humor, and integrity, and of incredible depth and talent. He is unique. I am fortunate that he was my creative mentor and so very glad that he is my dear friend.

Artwork by Mark Wheatley

EVEN DEAD BIRDS HAVE WINGS

IT WAS A PLEASANT RIDE DOWN FROM THE MOUNTAINS OF ONEONTA TO THE OCEAN'S SHORE.

AS THE POUNDING SURF BEGAN TO WASH AWAY ALL THOUGHTS OF TODAY, I SPOTTED A DEAD SEAGULL. JUST A BLACK SIL-HOUETTE FROM WHERE I STOOD...

...THOUGHTS OF YESTERYEAR APPEARED BEFORE MY MIND'S EYE.

I WATCHED IT RISE AND FALL SILENTLY AS EACH CREST BORE IT ON.

EVEN DEAD BIRDS HAVE WINGS

1942...ADMIRAL YAMAMOTO, MISINFORMED AS TO THE CONDITION AND WHEREABOUTS OF THE U.S. CARRIERS, BELIEVED HE COULD CAPTURE MIDWAY WITHOUT A FIGHT. WITH *100* SHIPS, IN WHAT HE THOUGHT WOULD BE A SURPRISE ATTACK, HE MOVED ON MIDWAY.

BUT AWARE OF THE ATTACK, STEAMING UNDER FORCED DRAFT TO INTERCEPT HIM WAS A *U.S. T/F* OF *33* SHIPS BUILT AROUND THE CARRIERS *HORNET, ENTERPRISE,* AND *YORKTOWN.*

EXPLODING ON JUNE 3 AND ENDING ON JUNE 6, THE CLASHING OF THESE TWO FORCES WOULD BECOME KNOWN AS THE BATTLE OF MIDWAY, A LONG-RANGE AIR ENGAGEMENT, A STUPENDOUS CARRIER DUEL.

ON OUR DESTROYER WE WATCHED AS FLIGHTS OF BOMBERS LEFT THE YORKTOWN. ELSEWHERE, FLIGHTS WERE LEAVING ENTERPRISE AND HORNET.

WHERE OR WHAT THEIR TARGETS WERE WE DID NOT KNOW.

BUT WE STOOD READY, ANTICIPATING AN ATTACK ON OUR OWN FORCES.

IN TIME OF BATTLE, SEAMEN ABOARD SHIP HAVE NO IDEA OF HOW BIG OR WIDESPREAD A BATTLE MAY BE...

...WE ARE ONLY AWARE OF WHAT WE SEE AND EXPERIENCE ABOARD OUR OWN INDIVIDUAL SHIPS.

NOT UNTIL MUCH LATER WOULD WE LEARN OF THE DEATH-BLOWS DEALT THE ENEMY 200 MILES AWAY BY OUR CARRIER PLANES... WHEREIN THE JAPANESE CARRIERS' KAGA, SORYU, AKAGI, AND HIRYU WERE TRANSFORMED INTO FLAMING CATAFALQUES.

SO WHILE OUR CARRIER PLANES WERE FAR AFIELD WE STOOD READY...

...IN FIRE ROOMS...

...IN ENGINE ROOMS...

...IN HANDLING ROOMS.

... ASTORIA AND PORTLAND, THE TWO CRUISERS IN COMPANY WITH US ALSO SCORCHED THE SKY, AS DID YORKTOWN'S AA BATTERIES.

OF THE 36 ENEMY PLANES, 8 EVADED THE YORKTOWN'S FIGHTERS AND THE ANTI-AIRCRAFT FIRE...

... BARGING IN, THEY SCORED THREE BOMB-HITS ON THE YORKTOWN...

... BEFORE BEING SHOT DOWN.

TWO HOURS LATER, WITH FIRES UNDER CONTROL, THE YORKTOWN WAS RECEIVING HER RETURNING PLANES. REFUELED, RE-ARMED, MORE TOOK TO THE SKY...

...TO CONTINUE THEIR ATTACK ON YAMAMOTO'S FLEET 200 MILES AWAY.

THEN "BOGIES" ONCE MORE APPEARED ON RADAR.

IN LESS THAN 6 MINUTES THIS FLIGHT OF 16 TORPEDO PLANES THAT CAME SCREAMING IN WITH THE USUAL CORDON OF VICIOUS ZEROES WERE CONSUMED IN A FURNACE OF FIRE SET UP BY THE SHIPS.

BUT FOUR HAD MANAGED TO BREAK THROUGH THIS CURTAIN AND SLIP TORPEDOES INTO THE WATER.

TWO STRUCK YORKTOWN'S PORT SIDE... BLOWING HUGE HOLES AMIDSHIPS.

LISTING AND REELING, THE GREAT FLAT-TOP SWUNG IN A HELPLESS CIRCLE AS ORDERS TO ABANDON SHIP WERE GIVEN.

GUARDIAN DESTROYERS MOVED FORWARD PICKING UP MEN SLIDING DOWN HER TILTED DECK.

YET SHE STUBBORNLY REMAINED AFLOAT, SOME OFFICERS AND MEN RETURNED IN AN ATTEMPT TO SAVE HER... THE DESTROYER HAMMAN, ALSO ASSIST-ING, SECURED ALONGSIDE.

MEANWHILE, 200 MILES AWAY, YAMAMOTO'S ARMADA HAVING BEEN DEALT A FEROCIOUS THRASHING, WAS RE-TIRING... LEAVING THE BATTLE.

SUBMARINE!! A DEAFENING THUNDERCLAP FOLLOWED BY A DEEP-BELLYING ROAR...TORPEDOED, THE YORKTOWN'S HULL WAS CRACKED LIKE AN EGG SHELL.

...SCANT SECONDS LATER, THE HAMMANN WAS ALSO STRUCK, LOWERING HER HEAD, SHE BEGAN TO SETTLE AND WAS UNDER THE SEA IN 4 MINUTES.

WHILE RESCUE OPERATIONS FOR THE MEN IN THE WATER WAS CONDUCTED, A HIGH-PRESSURE HUNT FOR THE SUBMARINE PROVED FUTILE.

MEANWHILE, UNABLE TO LAND ON THE LISTING AND BURNING CARRIER...

...... ORPHANED AIRCRAFT FROM THE YORKTOWN, RETURNING, SOUGHT SOLACE LANDING ON THE ENTERPRISE AND HORNET.

SOME BADLY MAULED IN THE ATTACK ON YAMAMOTO'S ARMADA...

...STAGGERED DRUNKENLY...

...SMASHING...

...AND CRASHING...

...THEY "FELL" MORE THAN LANDED.

THE BATTLE OF MIDWAY HAD ENDED... BURIAL AT SEA FOR THOSE WHO HAD DIED.

ABOARD ONE U.S. CARRIER, A DEAD PILOT WAS STRAPPED INTO HIS AIRCRAFT.

PILOT AND PLANE WERE GIVEN TO THE SEA... IT PASSED OUR STARBOARD SIDE... JUST A BLACK SILHOUTTE FROM WHERE I STOOD. BEFORE IT SANK.

I WATCHED IT RISE AND FALL SILENTLY AS EACH CREST BORE IT ON.

THE SHIPS, THE DEEDS, THE SAILORS, HAVE ALL SLIPPED OUT OF FOCUS...INTO ETERNITY.

SAM'S SCRAPBOOK

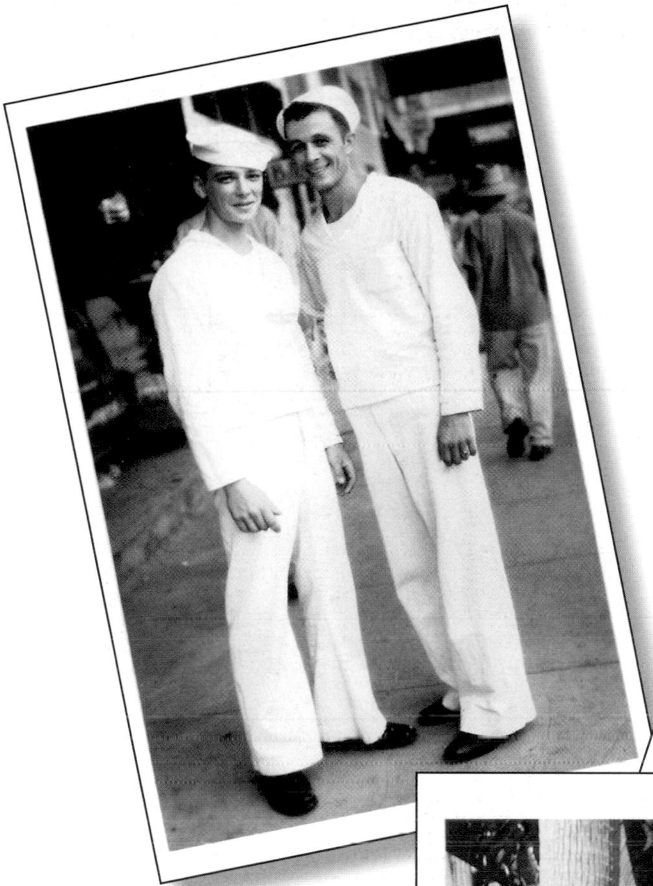

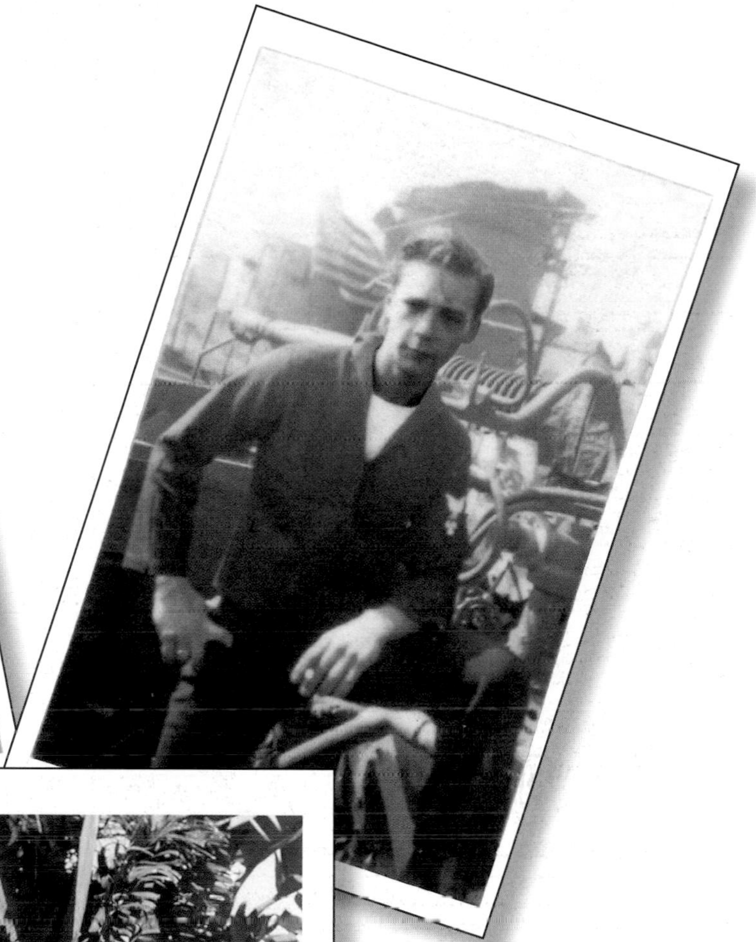

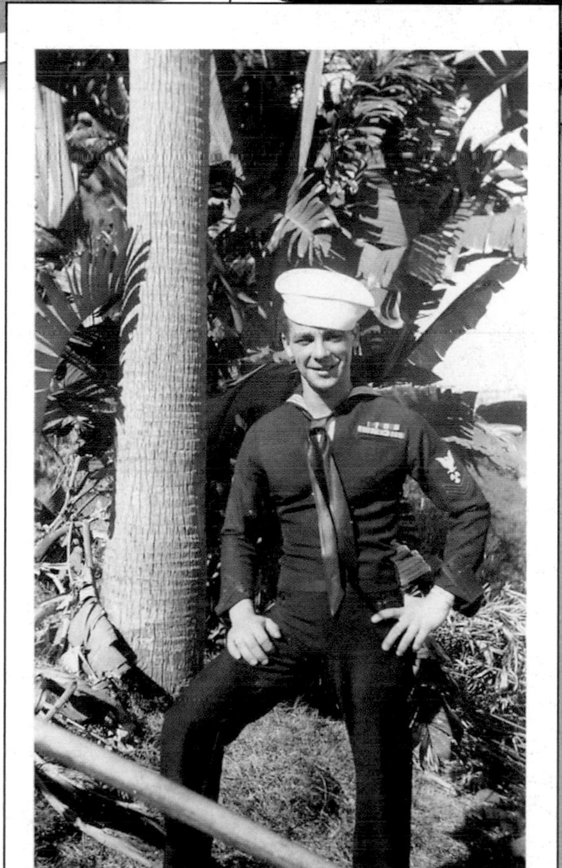

SAM'S SCRAPBOOK

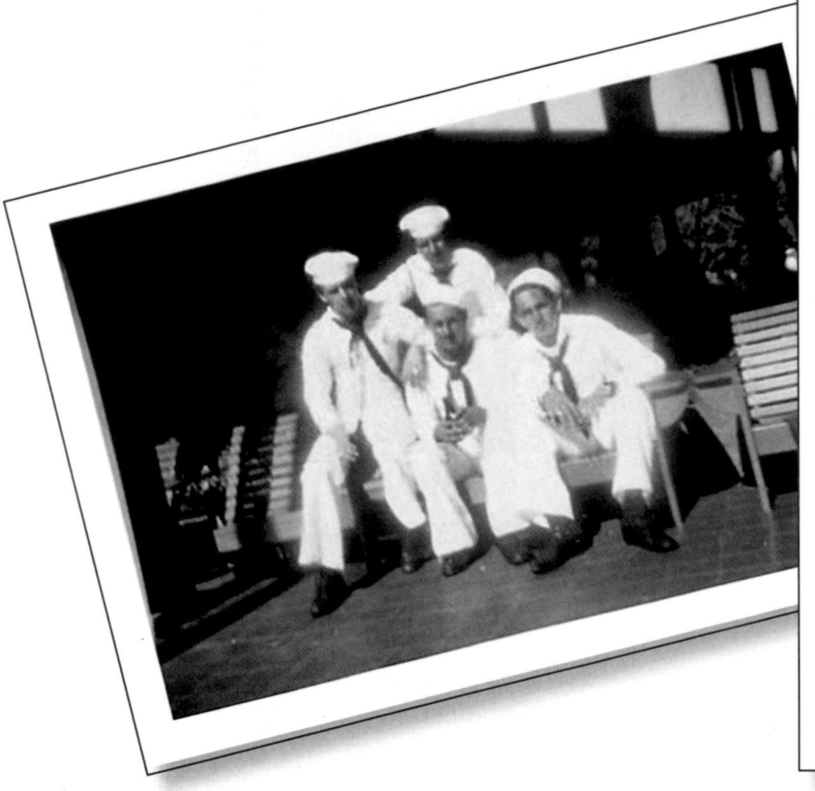

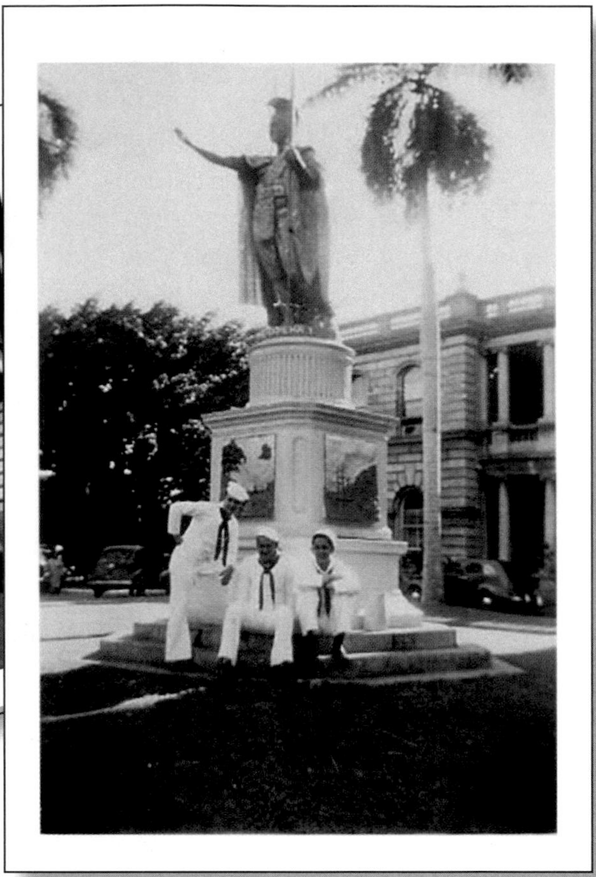

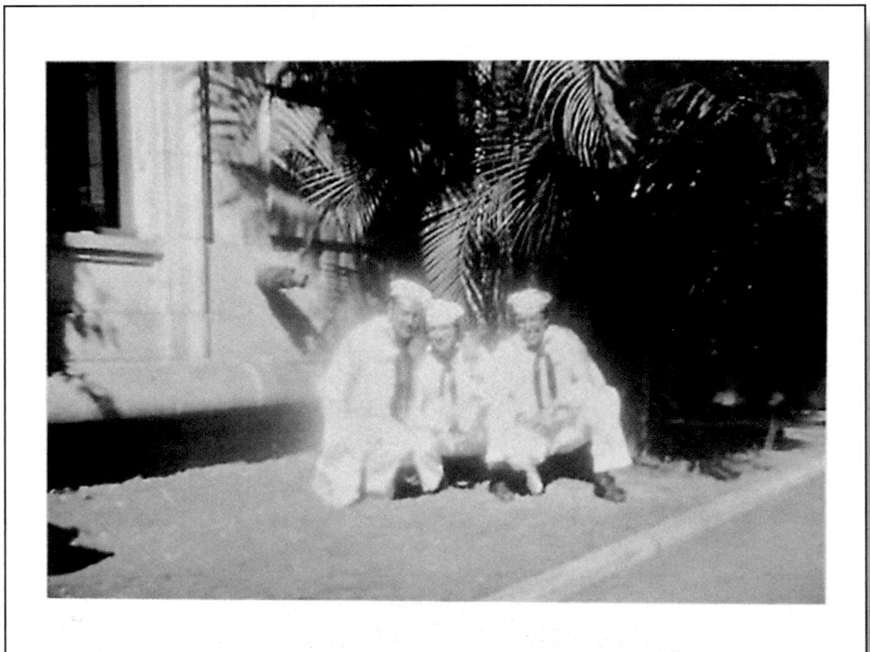

SAM'S SCRAPBOOK

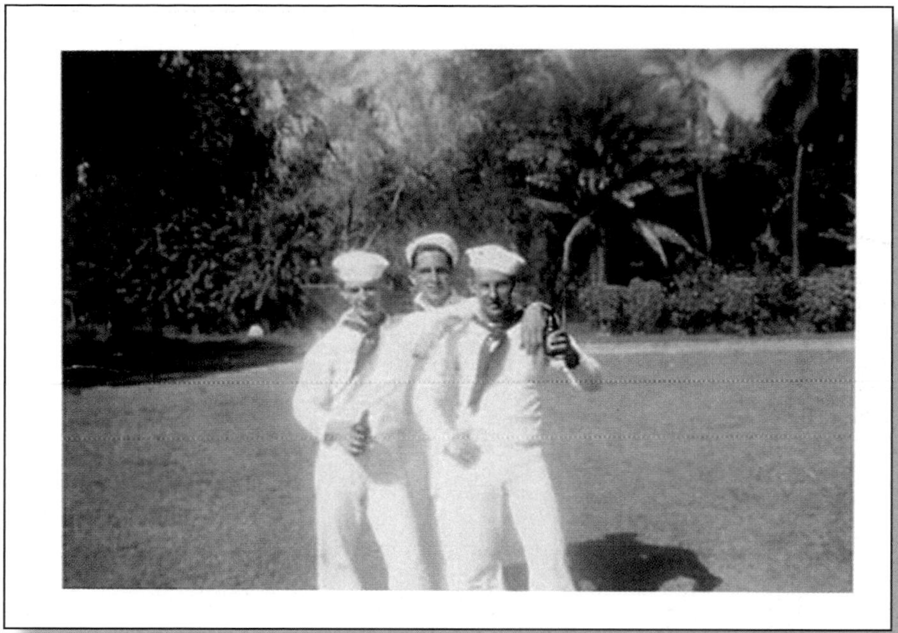

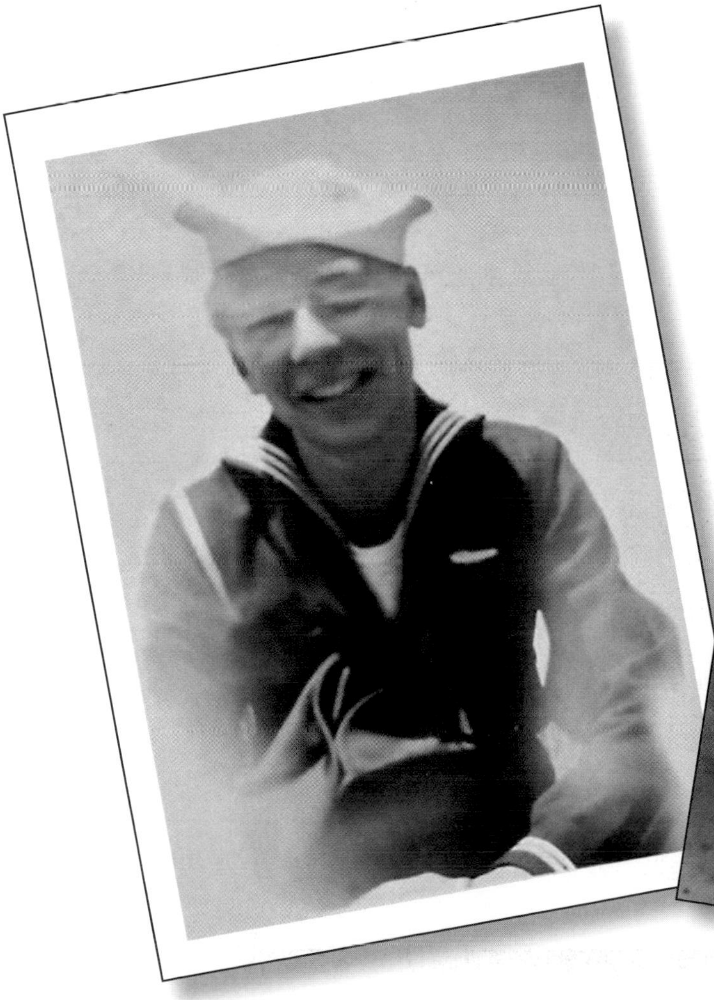

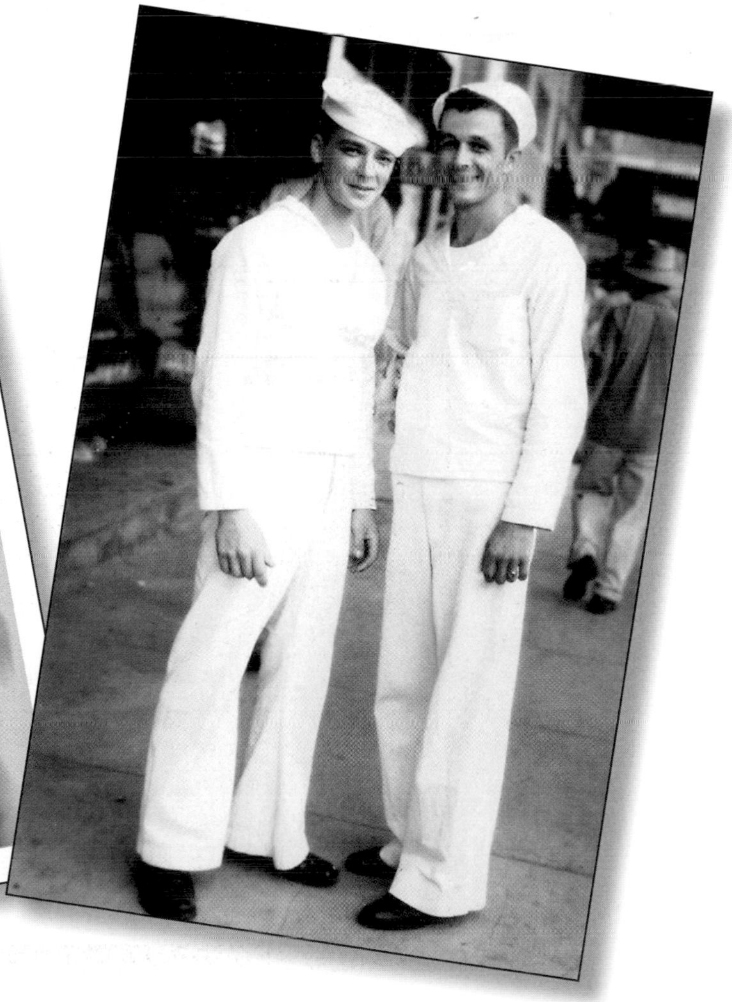

AFTERWORD
CHUCK DIXON

I first encountered Sam Glanzman's work as an impressionable young nerdling in the pages of an issue of a Dell Comic called *Kona*. The premise of the comic escapes me except that it had dinosaurs in it. And in the comic book in question there were LOTS of dinosaurs. Mr. Glanzman treated the readers to a sequence featuring a dinosaur stampede down a narrow ravine—hundreds of prehistoric critters of all types thundering and skittering and charging in a narrow-packed mob that threatened to crush the mighty Kona and his apparently helpless-without-him companions.

Those pages enflamed my imagination. And no wonder. It was an awesome sequence wonderfully realized by Mr. Glanzman. This was no parade of rubbery beasties trundling along like so many circus elephants. These pages were infused with the full chaotic horror of everything a little boy (or an artist of rare talent) might imagine if hundreds of primordial monsters ever got up to a gallop and decided to all head one way at the same time. I stared holes in those pages and re-read that issue often enough to have to repair the cover with (those obsessed with the grading of comics look away) cellophane tape. I also spent hours on the living room floor re-creating that marvelous stampede with my plastic dinosaurs and thrilling to the idea of the Earth shaking as they emerged from a rising cloud of dust toward me as they did on the pages of the comic.

It would be years later before I saw Mr. Glanzman's work on any regular basis again. I was a devotee of DC Comics' line-up of war comics. In the late '60s and early '70s those stories of Sgt. Rock, the Haunted Tank, the Unknown Soldier, and The Losers reached a creative peak in their development. They were more realistic and more mature than they had been in the '60s when the stories would feature massive fistfights more suited to superhero comics or gimmicky stories that were mostly one-note in execution. With Robert Kanigher, Archie Goodwin, and Bob Haney writing and guys like Russ Heath, Joe Kubert, and John Severin on art, the four war titles were serious comics taking the business of war seriously. They stood out among the crop of comics coming from DC and Marvel at the time as earnest works of sequential storytelling by seasoned professionals who were obviously taking the opportunity to present more meaningful, more impactful stories at a time when the superhero titles from the major comics publishers were in a sales and creative decline. Quite simply, these were the best comics on the stands at the time of their publication.

In addition to the lead features, the four war titles also has back-up stories. Most often these were one-offs about one branch of the service or another. Norman Maurer had an excellent series of stories about Medal of Honor winners. And Alex Toth created two of his most remembered stories (*Burma Sky* and *White Devil*,

Yellow Devil) in this period. John Severin offered the extraordinary two-page caption-less *24 Hours to San Francisco,* which is recalled vividly by anyone who saw it. But there was a back-up feature that was somewhat regular in the titles that stood out even in a pantheon of stand-outs. *U.S.S. Stevens* was a series of short comic stories written and drawn by Sam Glanzman, based on his own experiences aboard a destroyer in the Pacific in WWII. It was never plainly stated that these stories were autobiographical, but anyone reading them knew that these were not fictions. These were not simple action tales of rousing feats of derring-do. These were portraits of men in combat. As earnest as the material was in the lead features of the various war books, these stories of the *Stevens* were often a dose of the coldest reality.

Sometimes they were expertly told descriptions of action at sea, and, more often, tales of a single sailor. In others we caught mere glimpses of life on a fighting ship. There was dark humor in the stories along with real, never contrived pathos. These men knew fear and regret and loss. Unlike tales of Rock and Easy or Jeb Stuart and the crew of the Haunted Tank, you were never certain if the cast chosen for any *Stevens* story would make it to the last page alive. And very often they didn't. And, even though his allotted page length was short, Mr. Glanzman made you feel for those characters and made their travails real.

The *U.S.S. Stevens* had a remarkable run of over fifty stories across every title in the range. All told, they form an epic of their own. But even so, they are only part of the story of young Sam Glanzman's time in the navy. In *A Sailor's Story* you'll see more of the story told in first person by the man himself. There are no pretenses to fiction here. The curtain is lifted. Mr. Glanzman relates his own suffering and sacrifice and that of his fellow crewman in the Pacific theater without having to pretend they're just "stories." This is a man's life.